Extreme Science Careers

Forensic Science Specialists
Making Sense of Crime Scene Evidence

DON RAUF AND JUDITH WILLIAMS

Enslow Publishing
101 W. 23rd Street
Suite 240
New York, NY 10011
USA

enslow.com

Acknowledgments

I would like to thank Mark Lerner for connecting me to Jonathan Hayes, and I'd like to thank Jonathan Hayes for taking time to talk about his work as chief medical examiner for New York City. - DR

Published in 2016 by Enslow Publishing, LLC
101 W. 23rd Street, Suite 240, New York, NY 10011

Copyright © 2016 by Enslow Publishing, LLC

Cataloging-in-Publication Data
Rauf, Don.
Forensic scientists: making sense of crime scene evidence / by Don Rauf and Judith Williams.
p. cm. — (Extreme science careers)
Includes bibliographical references and index.
ISBN 978-0-7660-6962-6 (library binding)
1. Criminal investigation — Juvenile literature. 2. Forensic scientists — Juvenile literature. I. Rauf, Don. II. Title.
HV8073.8 R38 2016
363.25'023—d23

Printed in the United States of America

To Our Readers: We have done our best to make sure all Web site addresses in this book were active and appropriate when we went to press. However, the author and the publisher have no control over and assume no liability for the material available on those Web sites or on any Web sites they may link to. Any comments or suggestions can be sent by e-mail to customerservice@enslow.com.

Portions of this book originally appeared in the book *Forensic Scientist Careers Solving Crimes and Scientific Mysteries.*

Photo Credits: Abel Tumik/Shutterstock.com, p. 54; andrea crisante/Shutterstock.com, p. 11;©AP Photo, pp.66, 98, 107; Artem Furman/Shutterstock.com, p. 15; BSIP/UIG via Getty Images, p. 56; Christopher Furlong/Getty Images News/Getty Images, p. 18; Corepics VOF/Shutterstock.com, p. 49;Courtesy of Alison Galloway, p. 111; Courtesy of the Los Angeles County Sheriff's Office Crime Lab, p. 29; Courtesy of the Office of the Chief Medical Examiner, Calgary, Alberta, pp. 20, 27; courtesy of r.r.jones and the University of Santa Cruz, p. 97; Courtesy of Simon Frasier University, p. 47; Courtesy of U.S. Fish and Wildlife Forensics Laboratory, pp. 65, 69; Courtesy of VENUS Project/University of Victoria, pp. 59, 62); Courtesy of Western University of Health Sciences, p. 82; Dale A Stork/Shutterstock.com; p. 33; Dario Lo Presti/Shutterstock.com, p. 51; David McGlynn/Moment Mobile/Getty Images, p. 7; De Agostini Picture Library/De Agostini/Getty Images, p. 84; Fer-Gregory/Shutterstock.com, p. 31; Halil Sagirkaya/Anadolu Agency/Getty Images, p. 113; isak55/Shutterstock.com (chapter heads throughout book); ©iStockphoto.com/leonello, p. 90; John Elk III/Lonely Planet Images, Getty Images, p. 74; John Moore/getty Images News/Getty Images, p. 100; JUAN MABROMATA/AFP/Getty Images, p. 103; Iancu Christian/Shutterstock.com, p.78; ©Leonard Rue Enterprises/Animals Animals-Earch Scenes, p. 72; Lipowski Milan/Shutterstock.com, p.4; Millard H. Sharp/Science Source/Getty Images, p. 88; Monty Brinton/CBS Photo Archive/CBS via Getty Images, p. 9; photo-nuke/Shutterstock.com (fact boxes throughout book); Rafe Swan/Cultura/Getty Images, p.116; Repina Valeriya/Shutterstock.com, p. 40; Roberto Machado Noa/LightRocket via Getty Images, p. 76; Russell Watkins/Shutterstock.com, p. 34; SARANS/Shutterstock.com, p. 16; Science Photo Library -TEK IMAGE/Brand X Pictures/Getty Images, p. 115; Shawn Hempel/Shutterstock.com, p. 36; ©SNL/DOE/Science Source, p. 3;Visuals Unlimited/Louise Murray/Getty Images, p.44; ©Wilson, Marsha/Animals Animals- Earth Scenes, p. 68.

Cover Credit: ©SNL/DOE/Science Source (Forensic researcher).

Contents

1 A Tale of Telltale Clues 5

2 Death in a Dumpster 28

3 Bugging Out to
Fight Crime 46

4 The Case of the Walruses
That Lost Their Heads 63

5 A Dinosaur Detective 80

6 The Puzzle of the
Perplexing Person 95

7 A Future in Forensics:
Prepare for a Career in
Forensic Science 112

Appendix: Forensic Scientists:
Jobs at a Glance 118

Chapter Notes 119

Glossary 123

Further Reading 125

Index 126

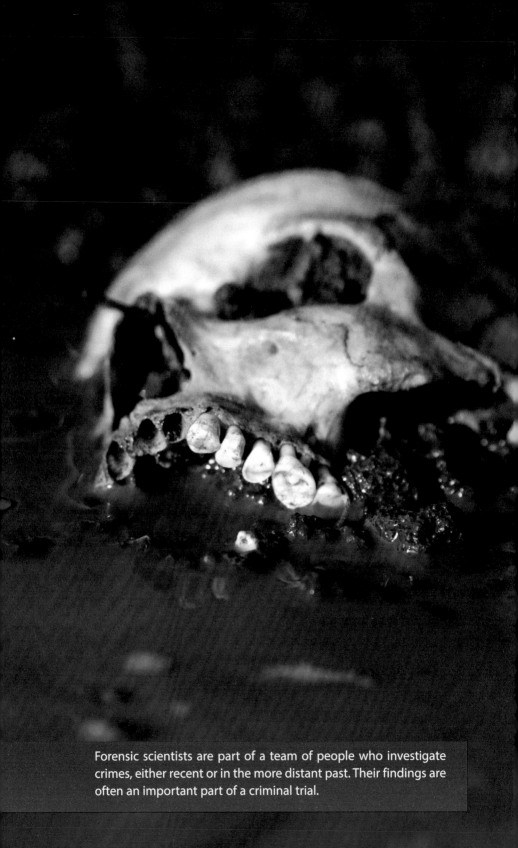

Forensic scientists are part of a team of people who investigate crimes, either recent or in the more distant past. Their findings are often an important part of a criminal trial.

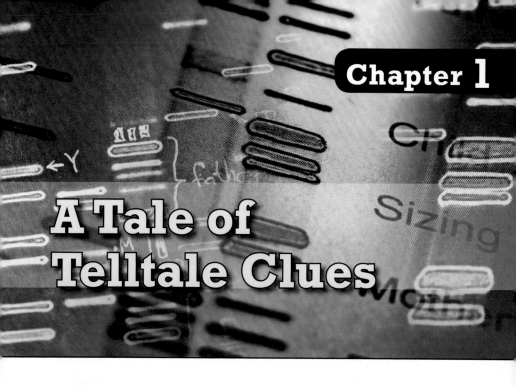

Chapter 1

A Tale of Telltale Clues

A seventy-two-year-old woman was found dead in her bed in Manhattan. She had had a history of heart disease, so at first it did not seem suspicious that a woman this age might die. But when she was seen by the medical examiner's office, some subtle signs raised cause for concern. The examiner observed a slight redness on the neck. Red dots were seen over the eyes, over the face, and inside the mouth. Although originally the woman was thought to have died from natural causes, these clues suggested that there had been compression of the neck.

As senior medical examiner for New York City, Dr. Jonathan Hayes said that this case demonstrates the type of work he does in the field of forensic science. Hayes is a medical doctor and forensic pathologist who has worked in the Office of the Chief Medical Examiner for about twenty-five years. The office is a branch of the New York City Department of Health and Hayes reports to the city's health commissioner.

Forensic pathology is a branch of medicine concerned with determining cause of death by examining a corpse. The findings of the forensic pathologist are often used for legal purposes. Medical examiners are highly trained in death investigation. A pathologist makes diagnoses by examining specimens taken from a patient. Hayes's mission is to investigate deaths in New York City that are violent, unnatural, suspicious, or unexpected.

As a type of forensic scientist, Hayes uses scientific methods to assist law enforcement in investigating crimes. Many people think his job must be as action-packed as TV shows such *CSI*, *Law and Order*, and *Bones*. While he does help solve some mysteries, the job takes long hours and serious research.

Fictional accounts of forensic science on television, films, and even in games typically gloss over the gritty reality of the profession. In real life, obtaining DNA results can take weeks. Scientists do not chase suspects down alleys with firearms drawn, either. Most criminalists do not carry weapons, even in major cities like New York. The stories played out on television have little in common with the day-to-day activities of the men and women who pursue forensics as a career.

While solving homicides to keep society safe is important, forensics is not always about murder. Sometimes forensics specialists will investigate a historical mystery. They may seek clues to events so old that the victim has been dead for a hundred years. Also, a forensic scientist may examine evidence in a suspicious fire or a robbery. In one case, a forensic scientist was able to identify a car thief from DNA found on a cigarette butt in a car. But whatever scientific trail leads to a career in forensics, the fascination is the same—using science to solve a mystery.

Hayes said that he came to his career almost by accident. "I kind of fell into this career. I started training

In his job as a medical examiner, Jonathan Hayes often works with New York City police officers and detectives to help solve crimes.

in pathology but the place where I was training was in the same place as the medical examiner's office. What I liked about the medical examiner's office was that every case had a story."[1]

When he realized he wanted to pursue forensic science as a living, he thought it made total sense. As a kid, he had been very interested in detective work. "When I was young, I used to go to the library and read books about forensics," he explained. "Ever since sixth grade, I was reading about the history of the Secret Service, the history of fingerprints, blood spatter evidence and things like that. Now I love the job. It's really satisfying work."

Factors of Foul Play

In the case of the seventy-two-year-old woman, the signs suggested strangulation, starting with the tiny red dots in the whites of the eyes and in the mouth. When hands go around the neck and compress the jugular veins, the blood keeps flowing into the brain and into the face, but the face becomes purple and congested during strangulation.

If the hands are applying enough pressure for enough time, the blood vessels become swollen with blood. Tiny blood vessels may pop and cause tiny red dots to appear in the whites of the eyes. These capillary hemorrhages are called petechial hemorrhages.

"They are a hallmark of a neck compression death," said Hayes. "You can see these types of little red dot

Real-life forensic scientists caution that the job of investigating crimes is not as glamorous as it may appear on television shows like *CSI* (shown here).

hemorrhages in the whites of the eyes and in the mouth for a variety of other reasons, but if you see them there, they are a red flag."

An Autopsy Gives a Closer Look

Having seen these suspicious signs, Hayes needed to dig deeper. He ordered an autopsy because some signs of strangulation are only visible by looking inside the body.

Before he started the autopsy, Hayes considered the possible causes of death. He put all the facts together that he had learned so far: the scene the police reported, the victim's medical history, and the suspicious red dots in the eyes and mouth. Hayes had a theory, but the autopsy would give him more information to determine if he was right.

To get started on an autopsy, everyone working on a body must use protective gear. A mask, gloves and gowns are universal precautions. The examiners are at risk of picking up a possible disease from the deceased person, so they take safeguards that are similar to those taken by someone who works at a hospital and deals with live patients. Hayes carefully checks the health records of a dead person to see if he or she had any infectious or transmissible diseases. Those performing the autopsy are extra careful not to cut themselves, which can expose them to such diseases.

A camera is always used to document autopsies. Photos may be taken by the forensic pathologist, the morgue technician, or a medical photographer if one is

Many different instruments are used during an autopsy—including scalpels, scissors, tweezers, and bone saws!

on staff. Many photos are required if the autopsy is for a homicide investigation.

The External Examination

The first step in the autopsy is usually the external examination. Hayes wants a head-to-toe examination, noting everything about the person's appearance, including height and weight; hair, eye, and skin color; and any clothes and jewelry. Once this is done, the clothes and jewelry are removed and cataloged. Next, Hayes looks for marks on the body such as scars, tattoos, or evidence of previous surgery, which are noted if present.

The second stage of the examination is to check for injuries. Many times during an autopsy, there are no injuries present because the death is due to natural causes and not homicide. This is typical for many places other than large cities.

In homicide investigations, documenting injuries like gunshots or stabbings is very important. Hayes will note their location on the body, their size, direction, and how they look. With gunshot wounds, he tries to determine the distance from which the weapon was fired. The forensic pathologist's task is to discover the cause of death, and in a homicide weapons are usually the cause.

If the decedent was shot or stabbed, Hayes takes an x-ray. Sometimes a knife tip will break off and stay inside the body. An x-ray allows him to locate the knife tip or bullet, remove it, and then keep it as evidence.

Looking Inside the Body

The next step is the internal examination. For this procedure, Hayes may be assisted by a morgue technician. Either the technician or the forensic pathologist makes the cut for the internal exam. Using a scalpel, the technician draws the blade down the body, making a cut in the shape of the letter Y. From each shoulder, a cut is made to the middle of the chest, forming the V of the Y. Where the two cuts meet, another one is made straight down to the pelvis. The skin is pulled back, revealing the tough chest plate of sternum and ribs. The plate protects the chest organs, and Hayes cannot see inside the chest cavity unless it is removed. To get inside, the technician cuts through the ribs using garden shears.

Once the chest plate is removed, Hayes looks inside the body for any sign of unusual internal bleeding. Then the organs are removed. Different pathologists have different methods for organ removal. Some remove all the organs at one time. Others remove them in groups by how the organs function; for example, heart and lungs would be removed together. Each organ is weighed, and this information is written down on a form. Using scissors and forceps, Hayes may examine and cut into each organ using a long knife.

To retrieve the brain, a special saw is used to cut the skull. It is the same kind that cuts casts off when patients have healed after breaking bones.

Hayes often dissects the organs to look for any signs of injuries or disease that might be clues to the decedent's cause of death.

Testing for Invisible Cause of Death

Sometimes the organs are diseased, but the evidence is invisible to the unaided eye. To check for possible diseases, Hayes may prepare a tissue sample on a slide and view it using a microscope. Abnormal tissue will indicate a disease.

When the examination of the organs is finished, they are placed back inside the body, the chest plate is returned to its place, and the body is sewed back up.

Blood is often tested as another way to find proof of disease. It is also used for the most common test done in the medical examiner's office—the toxicology test.

This test shows the presence and quantity of drugs and alcohol in the body at the time of death.

In the Case of the Strangled Woman

Upon opening the body, Hayes noticed areas of bleeding into the muscles of the neck, some crushing injuries of the Adam's apple, and some biting of the tongue.

"Then we knew that she had been strangled," said Hayes. "We then told the police we think we're dealing with a homicidal strangulation."

At this point in such a case, forensic scientists may scrape the fingernails for evidence. When someone is being strangled, it is often by hand. The killer is typically in front of the victim and using both hands on the neck.

In homicidal strangulations, men are more often the perpetrators against women. Men tend to have shorter fingernails, so they are less likely to leave scratches on the neck of the victim, according to Hayes. But the victims will often fight back.

Very frequently they will scratch at the killer's face or the killer's arms, trying to tear the arms away from the neck. In these cases, where there is close physical contact, forensic scientists have to be very careful looking for the transfer of evidence from the killer to the victim or the victim to the killer. There could very well be skin cells, blood, or bits of fabric under the nails.

"The old expression is: 'Every contact leaves a trace,'" said Hayes.

Fingernails can provide forensic scientists with helpful clues. If a vicitim scratched her attacker, the suspect's DNA might be found under her fingernails.

The Importance of DNA

Hayes and his team may also look for hairs or blood on the victim. DNA (genetic material) from skin, hair, or blood can help identify a criminal. If the DNA matches a suspect's DNA, they can identify a killer.

"You can also submit a random DNA sample to the lab, and they use a national or regional data base to find out if this exact same DNA material has appeared in other similar attacks," said Hayes.

In some cases, a strangulation in the Bronx may turn out to be part of a pattern of strangulations

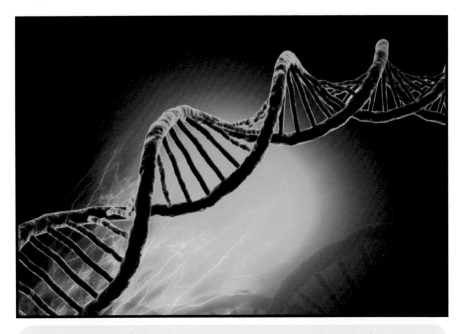

DNA is genetic material that is unique to each individual. It is made of two chains of nucleotides in the form of a double helix.

throughout the Northeast area. Once the scope of the problem is defined, it's easier to investigate the case to see what commonalities the killings have. This helps law enforcement officials narrow down who the killer might be.

Today, advances in forensic technology have improved how DNA can be used to identify criminals. To illustrate, Hayes mentioned a case that he started twenty years ago. A girl had been strangled and he found a single hair in her underclothing that did not belong there. At the time, a technique called mitochondrial DNA testing was just being introduced. This was an advanced method of identifying genetic material. The first mitochondrial DNA analysis helped convict a criminal charged with a 1996 rape and murder of a child in Tennessee. In time, the database of DNA profiles grew. Fifteen years after Hayes took that hair from the victim, a suspect was identified with the same DNA because of this mitochondrial DNA testing.

"The technology wasn't available when I started," said Hayes, "but years later we were able to link a specific killer to the crime."

Hayes pointed out that sometimes these forensic means of detection can help the living as well. He has frequently testified in court in cases where people have survived a strangulation attempt, particularly in the course of a sexual assault.

"Typically, these young women will have bleeding into the eyes," he said. "If someone is strangled and survived and the heart keeps beating, the blood will continue to flow through the burst blood vessels and so all the whites of the eyes will become reddened."

Not All Cases Are Murders

Like Dr. Hayes, Dr. Sam Andrews works as a forensic pathologist. He is also an assistant professor in the Department of Pathology at the University of New Mexico. He is often contacted by the police to explain a sudden and unexpected death. One puzzling case was particularly memorable.

Neighbors and the landlord had called the police when they realized that a young woman in their

DNA analysis, shown here, can help the medical examiner identify the suspect in a crime.

building had not been seen for several days. Everyone had been accustomed to seeing the young woman come and go regularly because she attended the local college. She had also been known to be health-conscious and went running daily. Because she lived alone, the young woman's sudden disappearance had everyone concerned. The police had been called to check her apartment to make sure she was all right.

The landlord opened the locked apartment for the police. The rooms showed evidence of the usual life of a busy college student: clothes everywhere, a computer, textbooks, and papers on her desk. There was no sign of the young woman, but the police noted that the bathroom door was closed and locked. After they forced the door open, they found that the concern of the neighbors had been justified. The college student was dead.

A Crime or Not?

Ordinarily, if the police find someone dead in a locked bathroom inside a locked apartment, they assume that no one else was involved in the death. In this case, however, the detectives noticed that the bathroom window was wide open. The window was quite large, so it was possible that someone had harmed the young woman and then escaped that way instead of using the door.

Since the window had been left open, the bathroom had gotten cold. In fact, the entire apartment had chilled to about 56°F (13°C). Although the woman had last been seen six days before, no one knew when she actually had died. A cold room can slow down how a body decomposes, or decays.

The bathroom was messy, but there were clues that this was not just an untidy room. Wet clothes were found on the floor and in the shower. The towel and toilet paper racks had both been torn off the walls. And by the window, brown-red streaks that looked like finger marks marred the white walls. Something unusual had definitely happened in this room.

The detectives directed their investigation to the woman's body. Her legs had been found in the shower while the rest of her body lay on the floor. Much of her

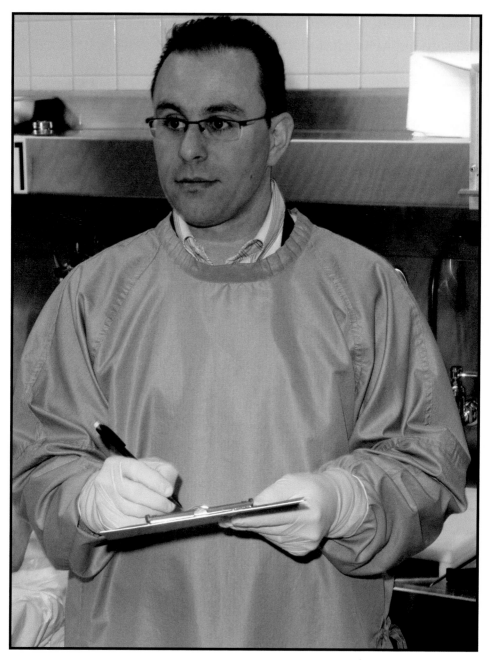

Dr. Sam Andrews is now assistant professor in the pathology department at the University of New Mexico.

skin had an unusual brown-red color and looked like leather.

The Pathologist Digs Deeper

How the victim died was unknown. Now Sam Andrews would join in and add his examination to the evidence.

Andrews needed a medical history. The only background he had at this point was that the decedent appeared to have been a healthy, fit young woman. He took a quick look at the body, noting the leathery, brown-red skin that the police had reported. It looked like a bad chemical burn. Andrews found it curious because it was not the kind of injury people normally get in their homes.

Looking at Medical Records

Medical investigators in Andrews's office contacted the decedent's family to find out if she had had any medical conditions that may have played a role in her death. The family reported that a year earlier the victim had been treated in the hospital after having a seizure. During a seizure, the brain's electrical activity changes. This can cause the body to do different things, including shaking or losing consciousness. Many different medical conditions can cause a seizure. In the case of the college student, the hospital had determined that the seizure had happened because she had drunk too much water.

We often hear that it is healthy to drink lots of water. However, like most things, too much is not only

A Cool Tool: Cut Proof Gloves

Cut proof gloves are made of a material similar to that used in modern body armor. These tough gloves prevent Andrews from accidentally cutting himself during an autopsy. He wears latex gloves, then the cut proof gloves, and then another pair of latex gloves on top.

unhealthy, it can cause illness—even death. With this young woman, drinking excess water made the salt levels in her blood drop too much, causing a seizure.

Medical History Holds the Answer

Since the examination of the body did not reveal an obvious cause of death, Andrews returned to the medical history of the victim. She had been previously hospitalized because of a seizure. Unfortunately, evidence of a seizure will not usually show up in an autopsy examination. However, the reason for the young woman's seizure had been documented. It had occurred because of low salt levels from drinking too much water.

The forensic pathologist wanted to test the salt levels in the young woman's body. When the patient had been tested for this in the hospital after her first seizure, a blood test was performed. After death, the best way to test salt levels is by removing fluid from the eye. To do this, Andrews uses a needle to remove the fluid. Both the eye fluid and the toxicology test blood sample were sent to a lab to be analyzed.

Because the victim appeared to have a chemical burn, Andrews took samples of the brown-red skin. Looking at the tissue under a microscope, he saw the signs of cell damage common with chemical burns. This confirmed his diagnosis of a chemical burn. The question was, how did she get these burns in her bathroom? Andrews believed the chemical must be in her apartment. He suspected that it might be a cleaning product—possibly bleach—that is commonly found in homes. He asked the detectives to return to the victim's apartment to search for anything that might have caused a chemical burn, particularly bleach bottles.

Bleeding in an Autopsy?

No, there is no actual bleeding in an autopsy because there is no blood pressure. Blood may leak out when blood vessels are cut, however. Autopsies are performed on tables that will drain the blood away from the body.

Back to the Scene

Back at the apartment, the detectives started their search in the bathroom. Andrews was right. There were two bleach bottles, one with the top on and one with the top off. Both were empty. Next, the detectives took another look at the clothes strewn around the bathroom. They were still wet, and they had the strong chemical scent of bleach.

Now Andrews knew the source of the burn. Bleach is a chemical that can be dangerous if not handled properly. But contact with skin is not the only danger. The chemical fumes bleach creates can make it hard to breathe. At least one bottle and possibly two had been poured out. The fumes would have been strong enough to make the victim's eyes water and to give her trouble breathing. She may have opened the window to clear the room of fumes.

But the real damage came from contact with the bleach itself. As was clear from the burns on her body, this young woman had poured it on herself, either by accident or on purpose. The burns covered 45 percent of her body. This was a very serious injury. As Andrews pointed out, "Your skin is [your] largest organ."[2] The burns alone were enough to cause death. But questions remained. Why was the bathroom such a mess, with the towel rack torn down and clothes everywhere? How did the bleach end up on her skin?

The Most Likely Scenario

The toxicology test showed that there were no drugs or alcohol in the young woman's system. The eye fluid test, though, showed that her salt levels were below normal. Based on her medical history, Andrews knew that the student had drunk too much water in the past and her salt levels had gone too low. Possibly the same thing had happened again. The changes this made in her body could have caused her to become confused and upset. She may have acted unusually then, doing things like tearing the towel rack off the wall and pouring bleach on herself.

The strong fumes probably made her rush to open the window. The fingerprints on the wall were most likely from her struggling to do this. The brown-red staining on the wall was from her skin, already showing the effects of the chemical burn. She may have suddenly realized the damage from the burn, rushing into the shower with her clothes on to try to wash off the strong chemical. Unfortunately, because of the combination of the low salt levels in her blood and the chemical burn, she had collapsed and died. As the forensic pathologist, Andrews determined that the cause of death was the chemical burns, but that the low salt levels in her body had contributed to the outcome.

In the Medical Examiner's Office

This case was like many that forensic pathologists see, with a combination of factors leading to death. On occasion, pathologists go to scenes of sudden death. These may include accidents, suicides, and homicides. In the morgue, they most often examine people who have died suddenly from natural causes—meaning a medical condition caused the death.

Sometimes bodies come to the medical examiner's office unidentified. If this happens, the staff go to great efforts to get an identification. They take note of any identifying features, such as scars and tattoos, that can help lead to an identity. Occasionally though, there are no unique marks to go by. Fingerprints and DNA are helpful only if they have records on file to match them to.

If the medical examiner's office has an idea who the dead person may be, the staff can see if there are any dental records to compare to that person. Using an x-ray machine, the forensic pathologist can try to match the x-rays to dental records of missing persons. But what if the victim comes in with no teeth at all?

The next step when trying to confirm the victim's identity is to check medical records. Perhaps the unidentified person had a chest x-ray taken in the recent past. If so, the staff then x-rays the victim and compares that x-ray to the one taken previously. Bones can be quite unique to each person. By comparing the chest x-rays, Andrews can sometimes determine if a missing person is in fact the decedent in the morgue.

Getting Ready for Court

Some forensic pathologists make appearances in court to explain autopsy findings in criminal cases. Before beginning testimony, a pathologist is often asked to explain the limits of forensic medicine to juries. This is necessary because television gives juries unrealistic ideas and expectations of what forensic medicine can and cannot do.

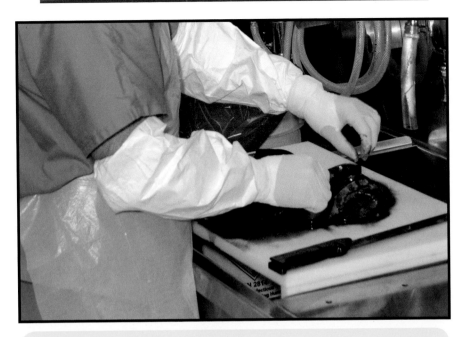

Dr. Andrews examines a human liver to look for signs of damage or disease. Forensic pathologists use the clues found in and around a body to solve the mystery of how the person died.

Forensic TV shows often feature a forensic pathologist plunging a thermometer into a corpse and declaring the victim died at a specific time. Some forensic specialists say that a body's temperature will drop so many degrees per hour after a person has died, so time of death might be estimated.

The real problem with TV forensics is that they make viewers believe that autopsies can answer every question about the cause of death. Sometimes, no reason for death is ever found.

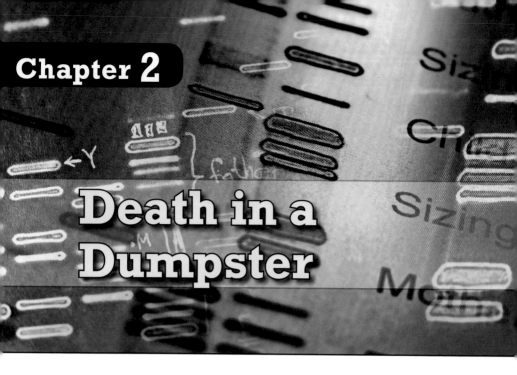

Chapter 2

Death in a Dumpster

Heidi Robbins is assistant director in the crime lab for the Los Angeles County Sheriff's Department. In a recent case, Robbins arrived at a crime scene and found uniformed officers and detectives in the area of a Dumpster. Robbins took her crime scene kit and camera, stopping to speak to the detectives who had called her to the homicide scene.

Robbins has a large crime lab team. Often specialists are called in along with Robbins to help collect evidence. Sometimes a forensic identification specialist (FIS) is asked to help document the crime scene, as in this case with the body in the Dumpster. The FIS would assist Robbins if there was a lot of evidence to be processed, particularly if there was blood on the scene. Together, Robbins and the FIS made up the forensics team charged with investigating this death.

Heidi Robbins is an assistant director with the Scientific Services Bureau Crime Lab at the Los Angeles County Sheriff's Department.

Don't Confuse Criminalist with Criminologist

Heidi Robbins is sometimes called a criminalist. A criminalist is the same as a forensic scientist, according to the American Board of Criminalistics.[1] By definition, criminalists are forensic scientists who deal with crime. However, it should be pointed out that not all forensic scientists deal with crime.

A criminalist is also different from a criminologist. While criminalists deal with physical evidence and science, criminologists look at social and psychological traits of offenders. They want to understand what motivates a criminal. They look for patterns of behavior with criminals to try and understand them better. They want to try to be able to predict what might cause criminal behaviors so crimes can be prevented. These experts

Looking for Evidence

As the people from the crime lab approached the Dumpster, they looked around carefully. Their eyes surveyed the area for evidence left behind. At the same time, they glanced up and down the alley for people who might be hiding. Although the officers had secured the area, it would not be the first time that a suspect returned to a crime scene.

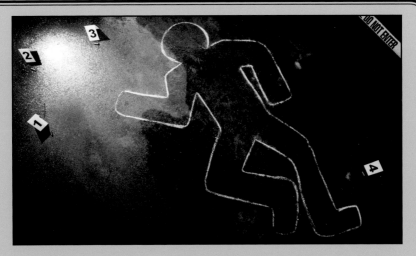

study psychological and environmental factors that may lead a person to crime. For example, a person who was abused as a child may take aggressive, violent, or illegal actions later in life. High unemployment in an area or poor quality education may contribute to illegal behaviors. Criminologists work together with other law enforcement experts to try to catch wrongdoers. Overall, their goal is to reduce crime and improve law enforcement.

Robbins is not a police officer and does not carry weapons. Even driving to crime scenes can be dangerous in crime-ridden parts of a city. Danger can sometimes be part of the job, and tonight, the forensics specialists proceeded with care.

Any object near the crime scene that could be evidence was examined. Then the forensics team began its analysis of the dumpster. The FIS took photos of the crime scene from different angles. The next step was to look for fingerprints. On a Dumpster there could be lots of them from many different people.

The FIS also had skills as a latent print examiner, a specialist in the collection and comparison of finger, palm, and footprints.[2] To collect the fingerprints, he first dusted them with powder and then put transparent tape over them to "lift" the print off the surface of the dumpster.

Each print was photographed at the same time. Then the tape was carefully removed and attached to a fingerprint card. The cards and photos were all documented as evidence. It was possible that none of the prints were related to the crime, but the FIS had to collect them to be sure.

Robbins took note of where the body lay in the Dumpster. The decedent was covered with blankets and several other objects. Among these was a large black rubber liner from the bed of a pickup truck. The liner helped hide the body from view—possibly the plan of the person who put the body there.

Dirty Work

Investigating a Dumpster is a challenge—and this Dumpster was a large one. As crime scenes go, this was a smelly and dirty location. Confronted with bags and bags of garbage, it was difficult to know what might be important evidence and what was not. The forensic scientist puts on a jumpsuit before investigating dirty

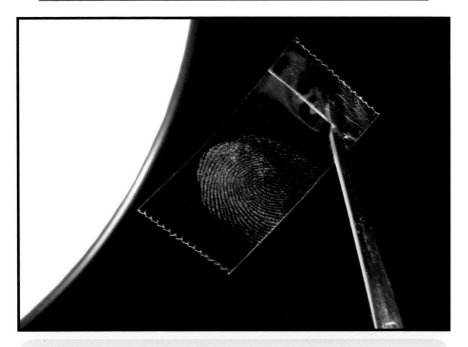

Robbins dusts for fingerprints and then uses tape like this to lift the print off for further examination.

crime scenes, whether it is to crawl underneath a vehicle, visit an arson scene, or climb into a Dumpster.

Robbins pulled on gloves to protect her hands from the victim's biological fluids. The gloves and jumpsuit also prevented her from accidentally leaving fingerprints or hairs of her own as "evidence" on the crime scene.

A quick look at the scene revealed something dark over some of the contents of the Dumpster. Robbins applied a chemical from a small bottle to the dark spots. This test confirmed that the spots were blood. The forensics team had to go through the evidence piece by piece. They were searching for any clue that might quickly give them information about possible suspects.

A Dumpster like this one contained all of the clues Robbins needed to help solve a murder mystery.

Once they returned to the crime lab, they would carefully inspect each piece of evidence again.

The FIS and Robbins next examined the items closest to the body. In this case, the victim had several objects stacked on top of her. They pulled out the heavy rubber pickup truck bed liner. There were indentations on it where it fit over the wheel wells of the truck. That might help match the liner to a truck later in the case. Most importantly, the rubber liner had blood on it, probably linking it to the homicide victim. Every object collected was photographed.

Robbins pulled several blankets off the victim. The blankets had bloodstains on them. One heavy wool blanket even had a bloody footwear impression on it. Robbins was encouraged to find that, as it was potentially a solid clue that could lead to possible suspects.

She also removed a large piece of carpet from the Dumpster. A bloodstain was on it. In addition, the carpet had a jagged edge, showing that it had been cut or torn.

The team recovered a wrapped-up, bloody towel next. They were curious because some kind of food was inside the towel. The food was white and chopped up in small bits.

A Calling Card to Murder

The Dumpster's next best clue was revealed when the team pulled out several pieces of paper. One of them was a business card advertising a tire retreading business.

This small business card carried important evidence. First, one third of it was soaked in blood, possibly the victim's. Second, the back of the card carried the impression of a partial boot print. Three lug marks left a distinctive pattern. (Lugs are the raised part of a sole that gives traction to a boot.)

Working carefully, the team removed the body from the Dumpster. The victim had endured many injuries, including cutting wounds to her right hand. People who work in forensics call these defensive wounds. Usually they are caused when victims try to defend themselves from an attack.

Staff from the medical examiner's office arrived to take the body to the morgue. At the morgue, the staff would work to identify the body and determine the cause of death. Meanwhile, detectives were looking for witnesses and speaking to people nearby who may have had information about the crime. The forensics team showed the detectives the business card. The detectives realized from looking at the address that the tire retreading business was in the neighborhood.

The detectives and forensics team believed the suspect dumped everything out of his truck that was related to the homicide, including the bed liner. Given the blood evidence and the business card, the detectives requested a search warrant for the tire business. A search warrant would give the detectives permission to search the tire

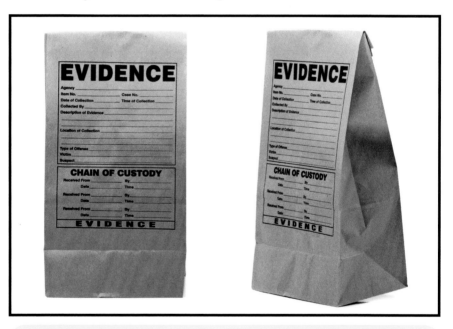

Each piece of evidence must be carefully collected and documented. Some items are stored in paper evidence bags similar to the ones shown here.

business and its owner for more clues. If the detectives found objects that might help prove their case, they could legally take them as evidence.

Meanwhile, the forensics team returned to collecting and documenting evidence about the crime. Robbins had to decide which of the objects they had found might be important to the investigation and which were not.

Collecting Clues

Kits for gathering evidence are quite simple. They contain gloves, bags, rulers, notepaper, and swabs. Forceps are used for picking up smaller objects or things that should not be touched, like the blood-soaked business card. Much of the evidence is collected and stored in paper bags of varying sizes. All evidence is numbered and recorded.

Evidence must be carefully stored so that it will not be lost. Biological evidence such as blood, saliva, and sweat must be placed in a container that will allow it to dry out properly, such as one made of paper. Usually, such items are placed in paper bags. When this evidence is dry, it is frozen for later study. Larger objects, like the carpet piece, are placed in cardboard boxes that allow the biological evidence to dry out. Items that are not biological, such as accelerants, are placed in airtight containers.

Sifting Through the Pieces

Small items—powders, fibers, glass fragments, hair, and paint chips, for example—are called trace evidence. They are collected in envelopes or bindles for safekeeping. A bindle, also known as a druggist's fold, is an effective but low-tech way of collecting evidence. Forensic scientists fold paper in several directions to hold trace evidence securely. They are limited only by the size of paper they have in their kits. The bindles and envelopes are placed in boxes for storage.

At the Los Angeles County Sheriff's crime lab, said Robbins, footprints are considered impression evidence. They are examined in the Trace laboratory. Evidence like tire tracks and footwear impressions are photographed by the FIS.

Detectives on the Case

The forensics team transported the remaining evidence to the crime lab for further analysis. The detectives got the search warrant they needed for the address on the bloodstained business card. Meanwhile, the body found in the Dumpster was identified from her fingerprints. Once this was done, her family was notified.

Outside the tire retreading business, the detectives spotted a pickup truck. A close examination of it showed that it had recently had a liner that had been removed. They could tell by the distance of the wheel wells that the indentations in the liner found in the Dumpster would match perfectly, and would fit the same model of truck.

Inspecting the truck, they saw bloodstains down the back bumper. The forensics team was called to collect evidence from this crime scene, too.

Signs of Trouble

Once inside the tire business, the first thing the detectives and Robbins saw was a bloody footwear impression. Its markings matched the pattern on the blanket recovered from the Dumpster. The lab would need to compare the two impressions to be certain. If they matched—and they seemed to—the forensic scientists could link that footwear impression at the tire business to the one found with the body.

The impression was an important part of solving this crime, but only if the detectives could recover footwear that matched. The suspect from the tire shop lived at the same location. The forensics team noted that the suspect's leather boots had a tread that matched the impressions. An examination of the boots also showed blood on both the sides and the soles.

When the forensic experts looked in the tire shop, they found spots of blood. Robbins said the blood pattern was "consistent with a stabbing."[3]

Robbins next found a piece of carpet. Like the carpet found in the Dumpster, this one was also bloodstained. The carpet had a jagged tear. Later, when the piece of carpet found in the tire business was laid next to the one found in the Dumpster, the carpet pieces fit together perfectly, like pieces in a jigsaw puzzle.

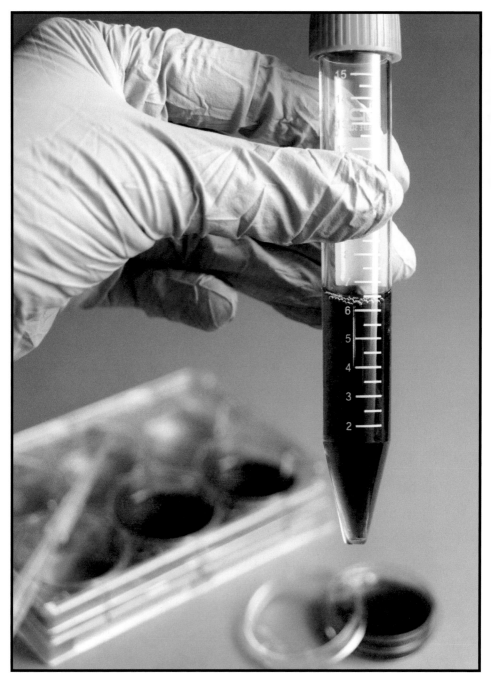

By testing blood found at the various crime scenes, Robbins was able to confirm the identity of the suspect in the Dumpster case.

The final piece of evidence was located in the garbage, a container with chopped white food inside it. Later analysis would match it to the food in the towel uncovered in the Dumpster: cole slaw.

The forensics team collected the boots and the carpet, as well as blood evidence and photographs of the scene. They were now ready to transport all of the evidence to the crime lab for further analysis.

How Blood Solves the Case

Robbins was responsible for all the blood analyses on this case. While this is just part of her job, a forensic scientist may specialize in analyzing blood and other bodily fluids. This type of blood specialist is called a serologist. Robbins performed tests that made the blood proteins stand out. Knowing which types of proteins were present in the blood helped Robbins narrow down potential blood matches.

In the years since this case, forensic technology has come a long way. Matching proteins in blood is considered outdated. Now, instead of identifying proteins, crime labs typically identify DNA types. DNA is the material inside cells that holds a person's genetic code. This code determines what makes each individual unique. DNA analysis is helpful for crime labs because DNA can be tested from blood, saliva, hair, and other parts of the body. But testing takes time. At the L.A. County Sheriff's crime lab, DNA analysis takes about six weeks.

When the tests from this case were complete, Robbins was able to match the blood on the towel, carpet, blanket, boots, truck, and the scene at the tire shop to the stabbing victim. That blood trail led directly to the suspect.

The Evidence Stacks Up

When Robbins was finished with the blood analysis of the leather boots, she passed them on to someone in the lab who specialized in trace evidence. In this case, Robbins performed the footwear imprint comparisons. She compared the imprints from the carpet and blanket, matching the tread pattern to the suspect's leather boots. Then she analyzed the three lug marks on the business card. Using a stereomicroscope, the Robbins discovered that the three lugs on the boots had unique characteristics. Identical marks were stained in blood on the business card. This proved that "those boots, and only those boots, made the marks on the business card."

A Cool Tool: Stereomicroscope

Microscopes are essential to forensic work. An optical microscope allows tiny samples to be viewed. A stereomicroscope has two different features: it gives a 3-D image of evidence, and also allows larger items to be magnified and viewed. Newer stereomicroscopes display images on a monitor.

Getting Ready to Testify

All collecting, storing, documenting, and analyzing of evidence must be done properly, or the courts will not accept it. Once in court, any evidence can be challenged. To prevent this, the forensic scientist and everyone within the lab must follow strict standards or guidelines. According to Robbins, "Forensic scientists undergo extensive training to ensure that they understand the methods [for handling and testing evidence] and the conclusions that can be reached."

One final step is taken to ensure the quality of evidence within the lab. All case work is reviewed by at least one other forensic scientist. With these procedures and safeguards in place, law enforcement officials can be sure that any evidence presented in court will be of the highest quality.

Presenting in Court

The final job for Robbins is to prepare for testifying in court. When she testifies in court, Robbins may present evidence before lawyers, judge, and jury. She has to answer any questions as well.

Robbins often has plenty of time to review all the materials associated with a case because it typically takes a long time for a case to go to trial. Her review includes all photographs, notes, and reports. As she reads everything over, she writes down the important details to remind herself of the different aspects of the case. Being able to confidently recall details in court helps a forensic scientist clearly demonstrate knowledge about the evidence. Now that Robbins has testified in court many times, it is much easier for her.

She explained how she handles appearing in court. "I used to be very uncomfortable speaking in front of people, which included juries. I used to get so nervous that I could hardly think on my feet. I found that if I memorized my court qualifications, one of the first questions you get asked, I could easily and smoothly recite them, which gave me confidence to move forward. I can't say I don't get nervous anymore, but the ability to be comfortable at public speaking is a skill that can be developed."

The pattern on the bottom of a boot like this was one of the many pieces of evidence Robbins presented at the suspect's trial.

Giving successful testimony in court is just one part of the many duties required to be a forensic scientist. The blood analysis and the evidence of the partial boot print on the card were good examples of the attention to detail that is critical to a career in forensic science.

In the end, this case was cracked because of the combined efforts of the crime lab team, those who went to the scene, and the forensic scientists who did the analyses at the lab. With such powerful evidence, the detectives built a successful case, and the killer was convicted for his crime.

A Challenging Career

Although in the past many forensic scientists did not hold a science degree, most crime labs now require one. Several colleges now offer degrees in forensic science, and many criminalists obtain graduate degrees as well. Students who want to pursue a career as a forensic scientist should be strong in such subjects as chemistry, biology, and math. Once working in crime labs, forensic scientists will continue to study to keep their skills and knowledge up-to-date.

Working as assistant director in the crime lab is interesting and challenging every day. Robbins said, "The best part of my job is being able to perform analyses which provide information to the detectives that answer questions toward solving the crime. Knowing that the work you did might prevent others from getting hurt is the most satisfying part of this job."

Chapter 3

Bugging Out to Fight Crime

When Dr. Gail Anderson saw the corpse, she knew it was a little strange. While the upper part of the body was mostly bones, the lower part was still clothed. The body inside the fabric was mostly protected, so the lower part looked newly dead while from the waist up it looked long dead. The skull displayed signs of a fatal gunshot wound.

Anderson was interested in all of these facts, but her examination uncovered the kind of thing that can make even experienced detectives shiver: the body was covered in masses of wriggling maggots.

When police departments across Canada are faced with maggots, blowflies, and a corpse, they ask Gail Anderson to assist with the investigation. Dead bodies, under certain conditions, attract certain insects. Anderson is an entomologist; she studies insects. She is one of the few forensic entomologists in the world. Because of her extensive knowledge about the rate at which bodies decompose and the life cycles of the insects that feed on them, she can offer the police critical information about time of death.

Forensic entomologists are often called to a crime scene if it is believed that the victim has been dead for more than seventy-two hours. During the first three days, the forensic pathologist can often go by police evidence and autopsy results to estimate the time of

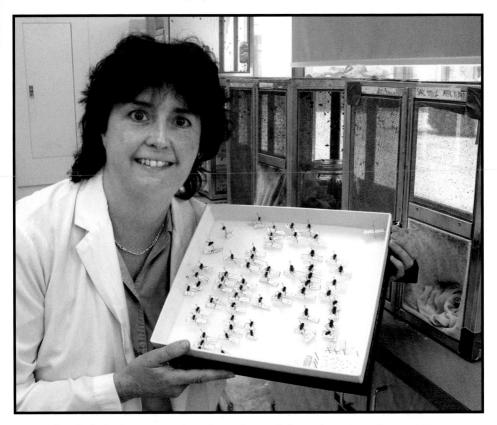

Dr. Gail Anderson teaches forensics and forensic entomology at the School of Criminology at Simon Fraser University in Barnaby, British Columbia, Canada.

death. After that, says Anderson, "Insect evidence is often the most accurate and sometimes the only method of estimating elapsed time since death."[1] In some cases, forensic entomologists can also be valuable in the first few hours after death.

Taking Precautions

When Anderson arrives at the crime scene, the police protect the site until she can examine the body. The detectives give her all the information they have, and then she puts on an officer protection suit to investigate the body. This police garb protects her from accidentally having contact with anything from the crime scene, such as blood or insects. The suit also prevents cross-contamination, so that nothing on her clothes ends up on the body. Gloves add to the protection. Investigators may not know if the victim has died from a contagious disease or if the victim is infected with a disease that could pass to them. Because of this, everyone is careful about contact with bodily fluids.

Another concern is the possible threat from the person who committed the crime. At the scene of a potential homicide, no one ever forgets there is still a chance that the killer may attempt to harm anyone connected with the investigation. Anderson explained, "The area is searched to check that the perpetrator is not nearby. . . Crime scenes can be dangerous places, and everyone has to be very careful."[2]

Protective clothing and gloves are necessary for anyone investigating a crime scene.

Once she reaches the body, collecting insect evidence is Anderson's first priority. If there are maggot masses, she pulls out her thermometer to take the temperature of each group of maggots. The temperature of the maggot masses gives her valuable information to add to her investigation.

Gathering Maggots We Will Go

Next, she collects insects from different parts of the corpse, taking samples from both on and underneath the body. Forceps are used to collect insects; a paintbrush is used to gently transfer larvae and delicate eggs into vials. Collecting the maggots, she puts half of them first into very hot water and then into a container of alcohol. The alcohol preserves them at that moment in their life cycle. She does this for two reasons. First, to correctly plot the time of death, Anderson must know the exact stage of development the insects were in when they were collected. Second, if the case goes to court, the insects preserved in alcohol will be entered as evidence.

The other half of the insects are taken to the lab to continue growing. Under carefully controlled conditions, they are raised to the adult stage of development. Some insects are much easier to identify when they are fully grown. If the insects are large enough and far enough along in their development, then Anderson can identify what species they are.

Sometimes Anderson is accompanied to crime scenes by her students in graduate school. This gives them the

Dr. Anderson collects maggots from crime scenes. Knowing what life-cycle stage the maggots are in can give Anderson a clear estimate of how long a person has been dead.

chance to learn how to treat a crime scene and to learn the skills required to collect evidence. Occasionally, if the crime scene is too far away for Anderson, others go in her place. These "identification officers" are police officers who have been trained by Anderson to properly collect insect evidence when she cannot.

If different species of insects are present on the body, samples of each kind must be collected. Knowing the science of entomology is extremely important for this part of the investigation, especially if others are at the crime scene instead of Anderson. For example, if someone unthinkingly puts beetle larvae in a vial with the fly larvae, they will discover that some of the evidence has miraculously disappeared! All the fly larvae will be gone, because the beetle larvae will have eaten them. Adult beetles cannot be stored with other insects for the same reason.[3]

The final piece of evidence Anderson requires is something that cannot be seen or picked up. The weather at the scene of the crime is important because temperature affects the development rate of insects. Anderson uses a datalogger to record the weather and temperature where the body was found. She will compare these data with the data at the closest weather station.

At this point, the body is placed in a body bag and taken to the morgue for an autopsy by the forensic pathologist. Anderson attends the autopsy to better examine the body. Often the best way to preserve evidence is to collect the body and bring it back to the morgue. If only bones remain, the body is examined right where it was found before being taken for autopsy.

Labors in the Lab

Once Anderson has collected all the evidence she needs, she returns with it to her lab at the Centre for Forensic

A Cool Tool: Datalogger

This small weather station records data to better understand the conditions around the body, such as temperature and humidity.

Research at Simon Fraser University. This laboratory is different from many such labs because it has police-level security. For evidence to be used in a criminal trial, it must remain in a place where it cannot be tampered with in any way.

Back at the lab, Anderson first makes a record of all the collected insects. Counting maggots is not for everyone, but for Anderson, it is just part of cataloging the evidence. She measures and examines each insect using a microscope.

Call the Blowfly to the Stand

Blowflies are the most common insect found on corpses in the early stages after death. These insects have an amazing sense of smell, traveling as far as several miles to feed on animal or human flesh.[4] Anderson said, "Certain species of insects are often the first witnesses to a crime. They usually arrive very shortly after death if the weather (i.e., spring, summer, or fall in Canada) and conditions are suitable, and often arrive within minutes in the presence of blood or other bodily fluids."[5] Knowing the life cycle of the blowfly is essential for understanding how Anderson estimates the time of death.

A Body of Evidence

Anderson plots each stage of development, based on the location of the body and knowledge about the season, weather, temperature, and many other factors. These factors determine how long each life-cycle stage lasts.

The Life of a Blowfly

Blowflies arrive on a body shortly after death, laying eggs in any wounds first. If no wounds are present, they do so in body openings, such as the nose, mouth, and eyes.

Each egg hatches into a first-stage maggot. This maggot feeds on the corpse and molts into a second-stage maggot.

The second-stage maggot feeds until it turns into a third-stage maggot.

When the third-stage maggot stops feeding, it moves elsewhere, usually into the clothes of the decedent or nearby soil.

The maggot unattaches from its outer layer of skin and waits until its new exterior layer turns hard. Its color changes from light to dark during this stage. After several hours, it becomes dark brown. This hard shell protects the insect as it transforms into an adult fly.

Days later, the adult fly crawls out.

The adult fly feeds, mates, and lays eggs, starting the process for the next generation of flies.[6]

Putting all of the information together is complicated. Anderson's experience and research give her the tools to accurately take this information and combine it with the necessary variables to estimate a time of death. "What we do is interpret the evidence that is on the body, and I give a minimum length of time that insects have been colonizing the body, which then infers the minimum time since death," she said. "So, I can say for sure this person has been dead ten days. It could be longer; it could not be less."[7]

Reading the Clues

With the case of the gunshot victim, Anderson took all the evidence she had to determine the stage of the insects' development. One of the biggest clues? The feeding frenzy of the maggots. The temperature outside where the body was found was 59°F (15°C). Yet, said Anderson, "Even after the body was refrigerated for two hours, the temperature of the biggest maggot mass was 20°C (68°F)." The extra heat from the maggot masses speeds up their life cycle. The warmer the temperature, the faster the flies develop.

Anderson went back to her research to plot the time of death. She calculated using the temperature of the site where the body was found and the time of year. Her research showed that it would take this kind of blowfly at least 9.3 days to reach the third stage in these conditions. Since the insects were collected on October 12, they must have been eggs on or before October 4.

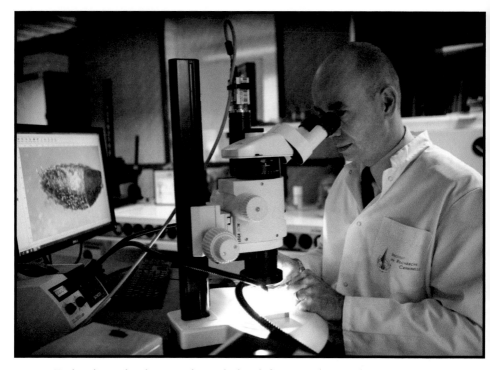

Technological advances have helped forensic entomologists in their efforts to determine a date of death. This scientist is examining an insect that was found in a corpse.

As there were open wounds on the body, and blood almost instantly brought these insects to the scene, she could conclude that the victim of this crime had died on or before October 4. In the end, additional evidence from the police proved that the victim had died on October 3.

Before the Judge

If a case goes to trial, Anderson may be called to court to explain the forensic evidence that she analyzed. She attends court as an expert witness—a specialist in her field. As a forensic scientist, her job is to show the role of entomology in estimating the time of death. Anderson must explain her evidence and what her research proves about the evidence. Most importantly, she must take advanced scientific concepts and make them understandable to the judge and jury.

Lawyers may challenge her evidence, and Anderson prepares for this. This is the courtroom version of "doing your homework." She makes sure she knows all of the current information and research that might be raised about her findings. Since Anderson is constantly researching how insects can show the time of death, she refers to these studies to make her evidence strong.

Anderson's past and continuing research is the backbone of any expert testimony she gives in court. With her graduate students, she has created a large database of the appearance of insects and time of death. Such information may be critical to a trial.

Bugs on the Body: Most Common Insects Found on a Corpse

Flies and beetles are the most common insects found on a corpse. Although blowflies are most likely to land on a newly dead body, the cheese skipper arrives a while after death.[8] This small black fly is most famous for the athletic abilities of its maggots. Using their mouth hooks, they grab the center of their bodies and spring up, jumping as much as 6 inches (15 cm) into the air![9]

Marine Animal Forensics

As a forensic scientist, Anderson also does research beyond entomology. Sometimes Anderson investigates bodies pulled from the water. Many factors affect how bodies decompose there. Water depth and whether any of the corpse is exposed to air and insects both play a part in her analysis. Anderson's interest in entomology led her to explore the effect of other animals that feed on corpses—marine life.

Human remains are frequently found in water. Not all of them are homicides. Anyone who lives near a river, lake, or ocean knows that reports of discovered bodies are not uncommon. Accidents happen all the time through boating and swimming mishaps, including drowning. Even plane crashes sometimes occur over water. But often, if a large body of water is near a crime scene, a homicide victim has a way of ending up there.

Predicting time of death is much trickier without blowflies and other insects giving clues to when the victim died. If a corpse is submerged in water, different creatures will feed on the body. But will they scavenge the corpse predictably, the way insects do?

A Laboratory Under the Sea

Anderson, who has investigated many such deaths, realized that forensic science could benefit from learning more about this subject. Not a great deal is known about the effects of decomposition in a body discovered in water. The types of creatures that feed on a body are

Gail Anderson with the Remotely Operated Submersible Vehicle (called ROPOS ROV) VENUS used to deploy and film the decomposition of the pig underwater.

known but not well-documented. Because of this, forensic science cannot reliably pinpoint a time of death.

A research project allowed Anderson to do precisely this kind of study. The Victoria Experimental Network Under the Sea (VENUS), is a state-of-the-art underwater observatory at the University of Victoria in British Columbia, Canada. The technology of the underwater lab provided a controlled environment from which to observe a corpse in the sea. As with many such research projects, a pig carcass (purchased from a butcher's shop) was used to stand in for a human body. The diet of the pig is similar to that of humans, so the way its body decomposes is similar, too. Even the skin of pigs is much like the skin of humans.[10]

Underwater Pig

The ROPOS ROV robot deployed a pig to the ocean floor. Above the carcass, a tripod held a camera to take photos and video that were transmitted back to shore by a cable. Although there were lights to observe the pig, they could not be left on because they might disturb the normal conditions of plants and animals that live near the bottom of Saanich Inlet. The lights were turned on at different times, though, so that video and digital cameras could capture the activity occurring on the pig.

The VENUS technology let Anderson view the submerged carcass on the Internet—day or night—from her own computer. Anderson explained that she could then see what kinds of creatures fed on the pig, and also "the types of wound patterns they produced. This is also valuable when human remains are recovered, as it gives us an idea of what marks on the body may relate to anthropophagy [feeding on the body] and what may relate to the homicide."[11]

Within minutes of being on the seafloor of Saanich Inlet, the pig carcass had attracted scavenging creatures. Crabs, anemones, and lobsters were among the first. Turning on the light on the third morning revealed that something large, probably a shark, had taken a bite out of the haunches of the pig. After this had happened, Anderson said, "Scavengers concentrated on the hindquarters."[12] The shark bite drew sea creatures to it the same way that blowflies are attracted to a bloody wound on a body on land. A small octopus and shrimp joined the feeding as well. After three weeks, most of the pig was stripped to the bone.

Anderson has conducted further experiments with her colleague, Lynne Bell, a forensic anthropologist, which looked at carcasses in other marine environments and seasons. This work has already provided information that can be used to interpret what sea creatures might feed on a human corpse, and the signs of damage they cause. Documenting the findings will make it easier for Anderson and Bell to scientifically prove what damage comes from sea creatures, and what might be the result of a homicide. Any extra evidence leads to a clearer understanding about time of death. Gail Anderson's

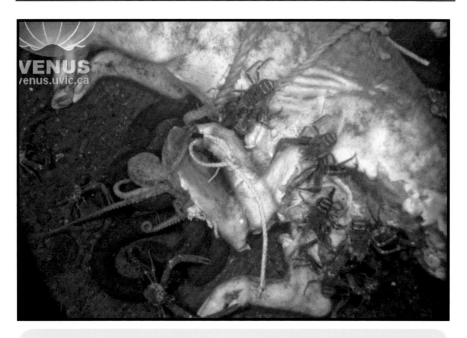

The pig carcass at the bottom of the Saanich Inlet gives scientists a better idea of what types of scavenging animals feed on remains, and how quickly.

work is important research that will one day help convict more criminals hoping to get away with murder.

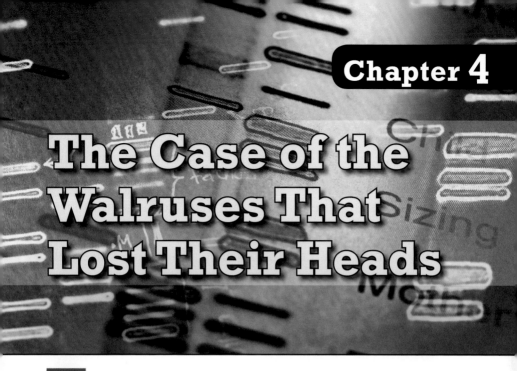

It's hard to picture. More than five hundred dead walruses washed up on several beaches on the coast of Alaska in the summer of 1992. Al Crane, an agent with the US Fish and Wildlife Service at the time, examined the bodies. He knew he had a case on his hands that required extra help—forensic help. The headless creatures brought to mind "The Legend of Sleepy Hollow." Like the frightening horseman, all the walruses were missing their heads.

The team from the US Fish and Wildlife Service Forensics Laboratory in Oregon were called in to help with the case. This was the largest laboratory for analyzing animal forensic cases in the world. One of the scientists sent to investigate the headless walruses was forensic chemist Dr. Ed Espinoza, the current deputy director of the US Fish & Wildlife Service in Ashland, Oregon.

Precious Ivory Tusks

Why were the walruses killed? Probably for their huge ivory tusks. The sale of illegal ivory from animals is a problem worldwide. The price their tusks can bring when sold illegally is high. The fact that these walruses were missing their heads, but had no meat removed, indicates that they were slaughtered solely for their tusks. Scientists refer to this as headhunting, since only the head is taken, and the meat and other useful parts are left behind.

Slaughter in Alaska

The investigation into the dead walruses began on the Seward Peninsula of Alaska. This peninsula is located on the Bering Sea. It was once part of the Bering land bridge, a tract of land that connected Russia to North America. Today, the Bering Strait separates the two landmasses by about fifty-five miles.[1] This relatively short distance between the two countries was an important fact during the course of this case.

As the beaches of the Seward Peninsula are remote, flying in by small plane was the only way to reach the walrus carcasses. With beaches acting as runways, Espinoza and other members of the team flew to the different locations along the coast, where the animals were rotting on the shore. They examined each dead, headless, and very smelly walrus. Espinoza paid close attention to the cut site on the neck. The exposed bones were bright white. To record this evidence, the scientists

Dr. Ed Espinoza is the deputy director of the US Fish and Wildlife Service Forensics Laboratory in Ashland, Oregon.

photographed each animal and documented details about the animals in notes.

While the team gathered evidence, they also took time to speak to members of the local native communities. Two main groups reside in this part of Alaska: the Inupiat and the Yupik. As a means of preserving their traditional culture, these groups are permitted to hunt walruses, as long as they harvest the meat. This is called subsistence hunting. If a walrus is killed, but no meat is taken, it becomes a federal offense called wasteful subsistence hunting. The native groups said they did not break the law. They suggested that the slaughter occurred in Russia, and that the ocean currents caused the corpses to land on the Seward Peninsula.

A Clue in the Currents

Espinoza and his team then needed to find out if dead walruses could float from Russia to Alaska. With fast-moving water and the short distance between the two locations, it seemed possible. Espinoza researched the way ocean currents move, and the probable path of the floating dead animals. After much study, he came

The headless walrus carcasses were found on the beaches of the Seward Peninsula, separated from Russia by only about 55 miles (89 km) of water.

to the conclusion that it was unlikely that the walruses came from the Russian side of the Bering Strait.

The origin of the carcasses was still unknown. The method used to hunt walruses complicated this problem. Native hunters were allowed to kill walruses if they spotted them swimming in the open sea—this is called pelagic hunting. More commonly, walruses are hunted when they are on ice floes. Usually they are shot, and then the meat is harvested from the body.

Espinoza shifted his research to where he thought the animals might have been killed. St. Lawrence Island and Gamble Island are nearby. They are also located along the route of migrating walruses. Hunters are more likely to kill walruses migrating in groups.[2] An examination of the ocean currents from St. Lawrence Island and Gamble Island showed that dead walruses would float from there to the Seward Peninsula beaches.

True Confessions?

Once the Inupiat and Yupik were confronted with the evidence of the floating carcasses, they changed their story. Yes, the native people admitted, they had cut the heads from the walruses. But, they said, the animals were dead when they beached on the Seward Peninsula. If so, then removing their heads was not a crime.

To prove or disprove the natives' claims, Espinoza needed a way to discover if the walruses had been dead when they washed up onto the beach. Espinoza believed that hunters had killed the animals out at sea, the heads

It did not take long for investigators to realize that the walruses on the Seward Peninsula had been slaughtered for their ivory tusks.

had been removed for the ivory tusks, and then the dead bodies eventually had washed ashore.

Proof Is in the Carcass

It is a fact of nature that some animals stay alive by feeding on the remains of dead ones. Usually, some life-form, whether microscopic or the size of a bear, will eat a carcass that is exposed on land or in water. Espinoza noted that the open neck areas on the walruses showed more predation than the rest of the carcasses.[3] Scavengers were more likely to feed on a new or open wound.

Although the walrus is a huge animal, removing the head can be a swift process if done with a sharp knife and knowledge of walrus anatomy. The skullcap of a walrus extends further down its back than that of most mammals. To remove the head, the neck must be cut low on the shoulder area. When the head is removed, the neck bones, called cervicals, are exposed.

On these walruses, the fleshy area around the cervicals was completely eaten away, probably by sea creatures. Because of this, it was more likely that the necks of the walruses were cut out at sea, not on the beach as the native groups claimed. To prove his theory, Espinoza needed evidence.

Espinoza examines a walrus carcass. He is holding a numbered card to help identify the carcass when reviewing photos like this one later.

A Closer Look at the FWS Forensics Lab[4]

Usually, cases are brought to the forensics crime lab by law enforcement agents, most often from the Fish and Wildlife Service (FWS). Espinoza described his workplace as "the only full-service lab for animals," because it has all the high-tech features of a human forensics crime lab, plus everything required to deal with animal cases, too. Each person gets to handle a case based on his or her specialties within the lab.

- The Chemistry Unit uses chemistry and instruments to test evidence, particularly related to pesticides, poisons, and unknown materials. It also does species identification and analyzes Asian medicinal products, which are often made from endangered species.

- The Criminalists Unit is composed of three sections: the criminalist experts, the firearms experts, and the

How Cow Bones Helped

To test his idea, a new research project was launched by Espinoza and his team. They positioned cow parts in three types of locations: the beach; onshore where the bones were exposed to air, but occasionally washed by waves; and in the deep ocean. Over the following weeks, they evaluated the cow parts. Those in the dry or alternatingly wet and dry locations still had tissue on them and were stained with blood. The stains indicated that scavenging was recent.

fingerprint experts. They examine evidence related to their specialties and also perform other laboratory tests, such as fabric identification and soil analyses.

• The Genetics Unit analyzes blood and tissue samples for DNA to identify animal species involved in a crime.

• The Morphology Unit analyzes body parts to identify what species they belong to. The unit is divided into three specialties of study: birds, reptiles, and mammals.

• The Pathology Unit does animal autopsies, investigating for evidence and cause of death.

• The Digital Evidence Unit analyzes evidence collected by cameras, audio recorders, and computers.

The laboratory working as a total unit allows these scientists to save animals and be on the leading edge of forensic animal science around the world. As Espinoza said, "One piece of lab work does not solve a crime. It is always a group effort."

The cow parts left in the underwater location were different. All of the tissue was gone, and the bones were white, without stains. This showed that the scavengers probably had arrived at the site shortly after the parts were positioned. The whiteness of the bones was familiar to Espinoza: This was exactly the way the walrus cervicals looked when the carcasses were found on the beach.

Over four years of testing, the cow parts showed that the bones left underwater had been picked clean by fish and arthropod activity. This proved that the claims of

Walrus tusks are made of ivory, which can be sold illegally at high prices. Native Arctic people have a tradition of carving and trading ivory pieces.

the native group were untrue. The hunters had killed the walruses out at sea or on ice floes, then dumped the bodies, which floated to the beaches of the Seward Peninsula.[5]

The Slaughter Continued

The US Fish and Wildlife Service Forensics Laboratory made their findings known around the Seward area. They hoped this would stop the illegal headhunting of walruses. But the motivation to make money from the valuable ivory tusks sparked a new method to hunt without getting caught.

More walrus carcasses appeared on the beach—headless, but with big slits down their bellies. Espinoza understood the idea behind the new plan: The hunters were trying to get the evidence to sink. Decay creates a great deal of gas within a carcass, making it float. By cutting the bellies, the hunters hoped the walruses would sink instead of floating to shore. But because the fat layer of this animal is so thick, the gas cannot escape. Eventually the hunters realized that they could not prevent the evidence of their crime from floating to land. Soon, in this remote area of Alaska, word spread that nothing the hunters did could escape the eyes—and science—of the authorities.

The research activities of the Fish and Wildlife laboratory made a huge difference. The very presence of Espinoza and the others, flying up and down the coast collecting evidence, discouraged hunters. In three years, the rate of wasteful subsistence hunting dropped from 84 percent to 23 percent.[6]

Risky Business

Researching a crime in a remote location can be difficult work. It is not like working in a city, where help is close at hand. One time, the unthinkable happened. Espinoza and a pilot were documenting walrus carcasses by flying to various locations on the shoreline, using the sandy beaches as runways. Strong winds during landings are one of the most difficult aspects of flying. In a small plane, the challenge can be even more pronounced. Along the

Seward Peninsula, the offshore winds are violent and come in powerful gusts. One day while landing, a gust hit the plane, tipping it into the ocean. Espinoza and the pilot did not panic, but quickly kicked out the windows of the sinking plane. As the aircraft went under completely, they swam through the frigid water to the beach.

They escaped one danger to face another. Being cold and wet on a beach in Alaska requires instant, common-sense decisions. Espinoza and the pilot knew the dangers of hypothermia, when the body's core temperature goes too low. Fortunately, they had a lighter with them. The beach was covered with dry driftwood, which provided plenty of fuel to burn. A search of their pockets revealed

Since the beaches of Seward Peninsula are remote, scientists had to travel by small planes to examine the walrus corpses.

a little bit of food between them, so they were grateful—the situation could have been far worse. They dried off and tried to get comfortable by the fire, realizing they could be in for a long wait before help arrived.

Twenty-four hours later, a rescue plane flew over them, a most welcome sight. After it landed, Espinoza and the pilot climbed onboard. Once they were strapped in, the rescue plane rolled down the sandy beach, picking up speed. Suddenly, the soft sand gave way, and the plane did a nosedive.

"Then four of us had to be rescued instead of two," said Espinoza, downplaying the adventure.[7] But this experience emphasizes that the pursuit of forensic science can sometimes have its risks.

Crimes Against Wildlife

Sometimes animals are hunted illegally, like the walruses in Alaska. Endangered animals are often the victims of crime, their body parts sold illegally or used in the manufacture of other products. Fish and Wildlife agents will sometimes send the lab a sample of a powder used in Asian medicine, for example, and the staff will identify whether an endangered animal was used in its production.

The specialists at the US Fish and Wildlife Service Forensics Laboratory use science to help catch suspects that harm animals in less obvious ways, too—such as poisoning them with pesticides. But the challenges for the scientists are daunting at times. Often, only small

Espinoza and the US Fish and Wildlife Service work to protect threatened and endangered animals and to bring to justice to the people who harm them. Shown here is the wood bison, which is considered a threatened species.

body parts are recovered. Agents bring them to the lab so that someone can identify the animal species. In a human crime lab, the corpse is always *human*. In the FWS crime lab, the only evidence might be part of a feather or a piece of skin. The scientists might investigate something as small as blood droplets—but from what? They could come from *any* animal, from a bird to a bear! The next step would be to determine what *kind* of bird or bear. Espinoza says both animal and human crime labs do have something in common regarding evidence: "They all seek to ask the same question: What is it?"

New Scientific Testing

As well as supervising a large staff, Espinoza ensures that any cases from the lab that go to court meet all legal rules. This can be difficult because sometimes the scientists need to prove that a crime was committed when there are no known tests to prove it. Scientists are often involved in developing new tests to prove that crimes have been committed against animals. It can be a challenge to convince a judge and jury that newly developed scientific testing is valid. If a case goes to trial, Espinoza has to ensure that the science behind the tests is solid and that no other research can challenge their results.

The Guitar Pick Case

The research done by Espinoza grows naturally out of the cases the lab is investigating. For example, a case was brought to the attention of Espinoza concerning the sale of guitar picks. The question was, were the picks made from plastic or from the shells of endangered sea turtles? Espinoza drew on his background as an analytical chemist. He analyzed a plastic pick so that he could re-create it in the lab. The pick was made from a protein called casein. By testing for casein, scientists in the lab could now tell the difference between the legal plastic guitar picks and the illegal ones from sea turtles. Those responsible for profiting from the death of an endangered animal can be prosecuted.

Espinoza used the scientific method to determine whether a certain guitar pick was illegally made from the shells of endangered sea turtles.

In developing a procedure or test, Espinoza follows the same rules for science that students use across country in their own science classes. A hypothesis is created, then tested and retested. In addition, the procedure and test must be acceptable to other scientists who look at his data. And sometimes, despite a great deal of time and effort trying to prove a hypothesis, no definite conclusion can be reached.

Is Animal Forensics for You?

Espinoza often meets students who are interested in becoming forensic scientists. He believes a student with an analytical mind may do well pursuing forensic science. Do you like puzzles? Are you a good problem-solver? Are you good at math? Then the analytical side of forensics could be for you.

Espinoza enjoys his work, but notes that it is not for everyone. Analytical chemists often work alone. If you prefer to work in groups, then this career may not be the best choice. He also does not want anyone to forget that becoming a scientist is a lot of work. But if students are prepared to work hard, a positive attitude can result in some amazing accomplishments in a forensic science career.

Even after many years in the field, the process of discovery still fascinates him. Espinoza said he is happy "when I'm working on an analytical problem and I find a solution. Usually I am alone, running samples, doing data set analysis, and can conclude things." The best part of his job? "Finding a scientific phenomenon that has never been described before." And in so doing, Espinoza uses forensic science to solve crimes against animals forced into an uneven battle for survival.

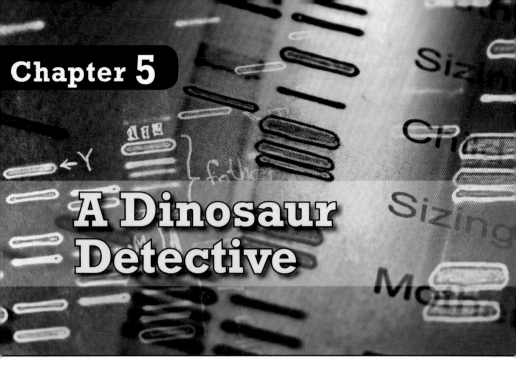

More than one hundred students had gathered in a large classroom. This classroom was a little different from most. Instead of being filled with desks, there were several gurneys holding dead bodies. The students gathered around the gurneys, and then carefully removed the plastic sheets that covered the corpses.

Dr. Elizabeth Rega watched the reactions of her students. For most of them, it was their first time seeing a dead body. Walking around the lab, she instructed the students in this unusual classroom.

The students formed groups, then cut or dissected the corpses as Rega advised them. The chemical smell was strong, but it effectively hid the scent of the corpses. Gross (large) anatomy is a required course for all students in medical school. If they are to become doctors, students must see the body from the inside out and three-dimensionally. By dissecting dead bodies donated to medical schools, students learn how body systems work.

Rega is an expert on muscles, bones, and the conditions and diseases that attack them. She paused at the end of one gurney, stopping to take a better look at the feet of the cadaver of an old woman. Rega took out her camera. Who would think that an old woman and dinosaurs, millions of years apart, would share something in common?

Elizabeth Rega is a physical anthropologist. Anthropology is the study of human societies. A physical anthropologist studies how life in a society affects the human body. Rega describes physical anthropology as "the use of skeletal biology to find clues to the past; a kind of CSI for ancient humans and animals."[1] How she applies this knowledge to scientific mysteries is amazing.

What Ailed *Chasmosaurus?*

Rega studies more than just humans. She is also an expert in paleopathology. This branch of science is the study of diseases and injuries found in fossils. Rega says of her work: "Paleopathology is like being a medical examiner, except that all the soft tissue is missing, the animals or people are thousands to millions of years dead, and the questions you are answering concern evolution, not crime. It's like being an evolutionary detective." Rega applies her knowledge of skeletal systems and their diseases to dinosaurs. And that was why she photographed the feet of an elderly woman in her gross anatomy lab.

The Canadian Museum of Nature had asked Rega to examine the hands, or manus, from two *Chasmosaurus* dinosaurs. One of the hands was not recovered, but

Dr. Elizabeth Rega teaches human anatomy and musculoskeletal biology at the School of Osteopathic Medicine at Western University in Pomona, California.

paleontologist Rob Holmes showed the remaining three to Rega. He hoped Rega could determine how the injuries on the hands had occurred.

Diagnosing Dinosaurs

Rega examined the bones closely. The fingers on the manus were normal. The bones were mostly smooth, other than cracks that resulted from being buried for millions of years. Strangely enough, though, all three fossil thumbs were deformed. Was this caused by an accident or illness? Rega looked at the three fossil manus sitting on her lab desk. The scientist knew that very few chasmosaur fossil hands had been found. Yet she had three hands and all had an injury in the same spot. The chance of two dinosaurs having the same injury was unlikely.

Rega reviewed what she knew about these particular chasmosaur specimens. They were heavy animals, and they were old. She could see that the thumb bones had grown unevenly as they had tried to heal. The injury had caused inflammation on the bone, and then infection. Rega believed the infection in the dinosaurs was probably bacterial or from a fungus. It would have been a chronic condition, meaning the dinosaurs had it for a long time, or it kept recurring. Dinosaurs lived pretty simple lives. Could the damage to the thumbs have been caused just by walking?

This is what scientists believe *Chasmosaurus* looked like.

A Human Link

Back at her office, the photographs of the human cadaver provided Rega with the example she was seeking. Hints of the woman's age and lifestyle were visible on her feet. Calluses and curved toenails indicated that for much of her life the woman had worn shoes that did not fit properly. And although millions of years and evolution separated a dead woman from a dinosaur, walking is something that caused them pain—because they both suffered from bunions. This is a common condition in humans, caused most often by a structural problem with the foot. Wearing shoes that are too small or high heels can also cause bunions or make them worse.[2]

Bunions become more common as people get older. The pressure of simply walking can cause them to occur. The problem does not start in the bones, though. The tissue that connects one bone to another to form a joint is called a ligament, and as people age, the ligaments move. When they do, the big toe bones twist inward. At the same time, the condition produces a bony growth on the joint of the big toe. It is painful—and seventy-two million years ago, was apparently endured even by dinosaurs!

Walk Like a Dino

While calluses may have shown that the old woman had worn high heels when she was alive, there was no soft tissue left on the dinosaur fossils.

This was not a criminal case, but in science, it is not enough to just state that the chasmosaurs could not walk properly. Rega needed evidence to explain why the dinosaur thumbs were deformed, because healthy animals are able to walk without hurting themselves.

The next step in her investigation was to consult again with Rob Holmes. She needed more information about how chasmosaurs walked. Rega and Holmes looked at research on trackways made by similar dinosaurs. From these footprints, scientists could measure the length of dinosaur steps and see how the fingers and toes landed on the ground.

Trackways are useful, but they are only a starting point. To re-create the scene of the "crime" or the injury, Rega and Holmes had to see how the chasmosaur really walked. How was this possible when the chasmosaur had died millions of years ago? They used the forensic evidence they had—the dinosaur bones and the trackway.

A Digital Solution

Holmes measured the dinosaur bones and created a small model of the chasmosaur. The legs and feet were positioned to fit to the footprints of the similarly shrunken trackway pattern. Every step of the walking process was photographed. Alex Tirabosso, the computer animator at the Canadian Museum of Nature, entered the data into a computer. . The result was a digital chasmosaur walking across the computer screen![3]

Rega and Holmes could see that the dinosaur walked with a rolling, side-to-side motion. Walking this way made the chasmosaur shift its weight, putting pressure on its hands and feet.[4] As these were heavy animals, this gait may have contributed to the damage on their thumbs.

After reviewing all the evidence of this case, Rega understood how the injuries must have happened. The chasmosaurs had suffered the effects of age, weight, and how they walked. Whether on human feet or dinosaur hands, this condition had the same effect—bunions—without the high heels.

A Very Special *T. rex*

The *Tyrannosaurus rex* named Sue is one of the world's most famous dinosaurs. Sue is unique because so much of her skeleton was found. An almost complete dinosaur skeleton gives researchers a far better chance for understanding the kind of life the dinosaur lived sixty-seven million years ago.

As scientists began preparing the bones of this *T. rex*, one thing was clear: This was a huge animal, 42 feet (13 m) long and 13 feet (4 m) tall at the hips.[5] Researchers pegged Sue at about twenty-eight years old. In the lifetime of a meat-eating dinosaur, Sue was just about as old as such a dinosaur might get.[6]

The *T. rex* Called Sue

No one knows if Sue was female or male. This *T. rex* was named after the woman who discovered her (or him!), Sue Hendrickson.

Decoding the Health of Sue

Most of Sue's bones are so well preserved that it is possible to see where the muscles attached to bones when Sue was alive. This very detail provided several mysteries for the scientist studying Sue, paleontologist Chris Brochu. His examination found several strange bumps, holes, and growths on the *T. rex* bones. Did these injuries cause Sue's death?

Enter Rega, with her brand of dinosaur CSI. An examination of the bones revealed the forensic mysteries to Rega. Several different bones showed signs of abnormalities.

T. rex Troubles

The first abnormality was on the lower leg bone, called the fibula. Rega examined the bone carefully. On top was extra growth that looked like a sponge. It showed that something was wrong with the fibula when Sue was alive. There was only skin protecting this bone. Because of this, any injury to the fibula would have been serious.

Rega wondered if the bone was broken, as this might explain the spongy growth. Scientists looked inside the fibula with a CT scan (an imaging method using x-rays). The CT showed that the bone was not broken. There was extra bone growth in one spot, where healthy new bone had formed over dead tissue. This showed something specific, a disease called osteomyelitis. Usually this is found after a trauma to the bone. Rega says that with Sue's injury the healing of the bone tissue took "months to years."[7]

Some animals might not have recovered from such a serious leg wound, but Sue was lucky. The other lower leg bone, the tibia, was not affected. The tibia is the stronger of the two lower leg bones. Because only the weaker bone was affected, Sue was probably not even disabled by this significant wound.[8] The forensic evidence is clear: the wound healed, so it did not kill Sue.

Bad to the Bone

Rega examined several other injuries on the skeleton. Two spots showed injuries and bone overgrowth from healing. On the first, on Sue's back, two vertebrae were

An artist's rendering shows a *T. rex* fighting two smaller dinosaurs. Rega's examination of Sue revealed many injuries, possibly from encounters like this one.

actually fused together from this kind of healing. On the second, on the tail, there was so much overgrowth that it crowded and left an imprint of the muscle on the bone!

More signs of Sue's rough life appeared as Rega felt a smooth hole on the dinosaur's arm and a smaller one on the shoulder blade. Her examination of the arm showed that the bone was not broken. The holes were probably signs of pockets of infection. Sue may have received a blow in that spot, or she was hurt in a fall. It's hard to imagine a huge dinosaur with pulled muscles and ligaments, but Rega said that would have occurred with such an injury. Because the arm and shoulder were so well healed, the trauma must have occurred early in the dinosaur's life.

Cracked Ribs

The next abnormality was several cracked ribs. Oddly enough, the bone overgrowth formed a line across the side of Sue's body. This suggested that all the ribs suffered a trauma at the same time. The site showed a unique healing pattern Rega recognized from birds and mammals. First, blood had gathered around the injury. The tissue had thickened, then bone had grown over the break. This told Rega that Sue had healthy healing on the ribs. The scientist noted another factor: one of the ribs had a split in the middle, almost like a hinge. Rega knew this could occur if the bone had continued to move during healing. Considering the location of the ribs, the bone may have kept moving simply because of Sue's normal breathing.

Battle Scars?

Of all the abnormalities on the *T. rex*, scientists were most interested in the damage on Sue's skull. Along the dinosaur's lower jaw was a series of holes. Were they bite marks? Was Sue once involved in a battle with another dinosaur?

There is skeletal evidence that face biting existed within the dinosaur world. When one animal bites another, the teeth leave a pattern, both side to side and up and down as the upper and lower jaws apply biting force. Face biting in dinosaurs took two forms. The first kind occurred when dinosaurs of different species fought each other. The second kind occurred when two dinosaurs of the same species competed for mates, prey, or territory.

Meat-eating dinosaurs were not known for their good manners. They roughly tore the flesh off their prey, dragging their teeth over muscle and bone. Millions of years later, those raking marks remain visible on fossils. If you bite into an apple without withdrawing any of the flesh, your teeth will leave a neat pattern. But if the apple is hanging off a string when you bite it, your teeth may leave a raking pattern instead. It is harder to bite a moving object!

Face biting seemed to be the logical explanation for the holes on Sue's face. Rega, however, found several clues that seemed to disprove this theory. First, she noted that the holes did not have a jaw bite pattern. Second, she could see that the holes had healed at different times. This indicated that whatever formed them did not occur all at once. Third, the holes were in a place where it would be hard to bite a dinosaur—at the back of the lower jaw, almost into the neck. Finally, similar holes exist in almost every "old" *T. rex* that has been found, as well as in other meat-eating dinosaurs.

These factors led Rega to believe that the holes were the result of an illness that Sue lived with for a very long time. It may have been caused by bacteria or a fungus. Mouths usually contain such things, but in a healthy balance. If one kind of bacterium or fungus grew in excess, then it may have been enough to cause damage. Probably the infection started with sores, and then progressed to eating right into the jawbone, eventually leaving its "evidence" in the form of holes. Rega stated that it was possible that whatever caused this illness may not even exist now.

Autopsy for a Giant

There is no way to be certain that diseases that existed millions of years ago were similar to ones animals experience today. But with animals, bones are bones. Even though dinosaurs lived so long ago, and seem so different from humans, there is still a great deal of similarity in the way they healed from disease or trauma.

After examining the evidence from the *T. rex* autopsy, Rega was willing to make an educated forensic guess about how these injuries played into the death of Sue. Her conclusion? The reason for death was not evident on the skeleton. There were plenty of injuries and infection damage visible on the bones of this old dinosaur, but they had all happened at different times, and all were healing or had healed. Sue's skeleton held the clues to a rough life, tangled with accidents and illness, but these events were not the cause of her death. Instead, said Rega, "Sue was a healthy animal dealing with life's insults."[9] Just as the world of human forensic science cannot always find a satisfying answer, Sue's cause of death remains a mystery.

Cracking a Million-Year-Old Case

Paleopathology is a relatively new field in forensic science. For scientists like Rega, this field is a challenge because it is not always easy to figure out what diseases and types of healing happened in animals that are extinct. In addition, it is still quite rare to discover fossils with abnormalities. The more these unusual finds are made and studied, the more we will understand about ancient injuries and illness. Fortunately for paleontologists, Rega's background in physical anthropology and skeletal biology are a perfect match to help discover the past lives—and mishaps—of dinosaurs.

Rega finds her career in paleopathology rewarding. She explained, "I was excited to use the opportunity to do good science in the field," because as a physical anthropologist she can provide different ideas to explain how injuries and diseases appear in fossils. But her work on dinosaurs offers something more. Rega said it is "a new line of evidence to understand evolution and behavior."[10] Discovering new scientific facts is fascinating work, and one where forensic CSI can go back in time, even millions of years, to solve a case.

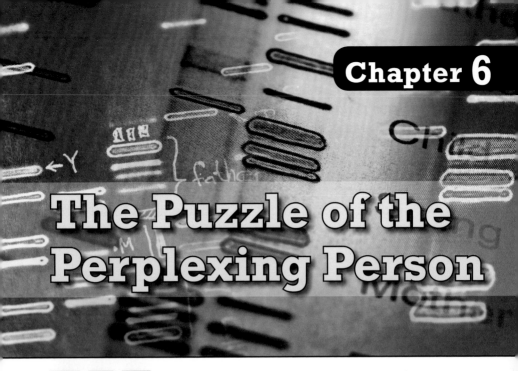

Chapter 6

The Puzzle of the Perplexing Person

When human remains were discovered in the Santa Cruz Mountains of California, Dr. Alison Galloway got a call. Workers with a steam train that regularly traveled through this area had uncovered the remains. They thought the circumstances could be suspicious. In particular, they had found a hole in the skull. Galloway rushed to join the coroners and sheriff, intrigued about the body that had been unearthed.

Galloway is a forensic anthropologist, and human bones are her specialty. Accustomed to crime scenes, she surveyed the site before her eyes settled on the body itself. There was no soft tissue left on the skeleton. The bones had traces of roots and fungus on them, hinting that the body had been there for many years.

Galloway described the scene: "The body was laid out on its back, the skull rolled a bit to one side as if someone had picked it up. As the leaf cover was cleared away, items were also found. These included a toothbrush, a comb, a whiskey bottle, a gold pocket watch, and a revolver with a spent bullet. It was very apparent that the person had been there a long time."[1] All of these objects were very old. The items might be valuable clues to solve the mystery of when this person died, and how.

A Fallen Fellow?

Before the body could be moved, Galloway had to document the way it was found. She cleared away all the debris, then photographed and made a sketch of how the body lay on the ground. She wrote all known details in a report.

One of the first things that interested Galloway was the presence of several coins found with the body. The newest ones were dated 1892, so the body had probably been there since at least that time. Because the remains had been exposed for more than a hundred years, Galloway was surprised they were in such good condition.

Sometimes first impressions are valuable, so Galloway considered how this individual might have died based on the evidence right in front of her. The whiskey bottle provided one possible explanation. Did this person have too much to drink? If so, he or she could have lain down on the forest floor, not noticing that it was too cold or hot.

Despite the concerns of the workers who found the body, Galloway did not see anything unusual about the skull. She would examine it more closely once the remains were moved to her laboratory. For now, nothing in the evidence suggested an obvious cause of death.

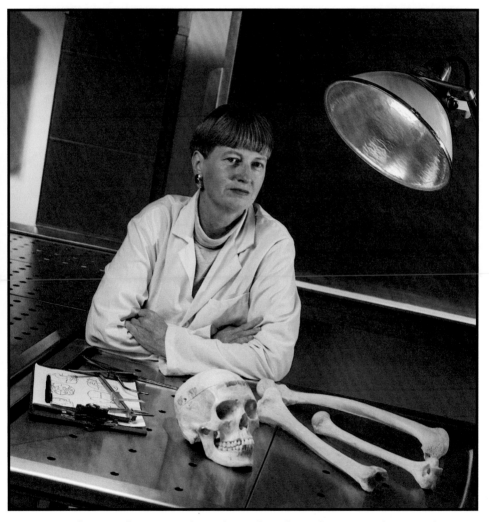

Dr. Alison Galloway teaches physical anthropology, osteology, and forensic anthropology at the University of Southern California, Santa Cruz.

Mysterious remains were found in the Santa Cruz Mountains, shown here. Galloway was called in to investigate.

One thing caught her eye, though. At some point in the victim's life, he or she had suffered a broken leg. The bones show that it had healed very well.

The body was transported to the morgue for the pathologist or medical examiner's examination. Once that was done, it could be transported to Galloway's lab. There, graduate student researchers would help her prepare the body for study.

The Lovely Bones

The first task was to clean the bones. If there is any flesh left on a skeleton, it must be cut and removed. Since all flesh cannot be removed by this method, the team must boil the bones until they are clean enough to show damage, which is "generally a very messy and smelly process," according to Galloway. Once the bones are boiled, they use forceps, scissors, and scalpels to remove any flesh that remains.

Luckily in this case, the bones did not have any flesh remaining. All Galloway needed to do was brush off the dirt and leaves. Next, the bones were laid out and organized as they would have been in life. Fortunately, many of the bones were recovered. Students counted them to see which bones were present and which ones were missing.

Galloway's expertise in physical anthropology was helpful for the next step in forensic analysis, called the "biological profile." This part of the examination would help identify the body.

Usually Galloway begins by determining if the skeleton is male or female. To do this, she also considers the evidence with the body, where it was found, and the habits of people a hundred years ago. Since the body was found in the woods with a whiskey bottle, a gun, and coins, this hinted more at a man's activities than those of a woman.

An Unexpected Find

Next, the team took measurements of the various bones. For the long bones, a bone board was used. It has a sliding scale to measure the sizes of the bones. Calipers,

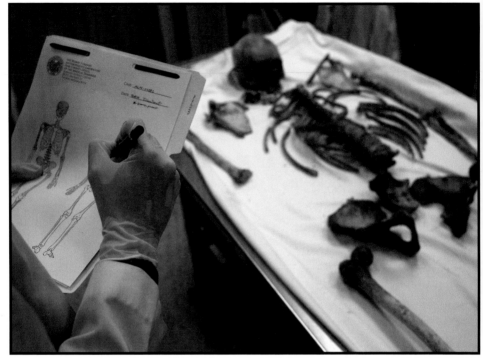

A forensic anthropologist takes inventory of skeletal remains. Galloway performed a similar procedure in her attempt to identify the mystery skeleton found in the mountains.

a set of arms that open and close, are used to measure bones as well.

Galloway explained her findings from the skeleton: "The circumstances of this case strongly suggested male, but when we looked at the bones we were surprised to find that many of the features we use to determine sex were actually female. The best area to determine sex is the front of the pelvis, but that was missing due to weathering of the bone. The back part of the pelvis had a wide notch, which we usually see in females, and the lengths of the long bones were more characteristic of female than male. The joint sizes were also not clearly male or female."

Evidence at this point leaned toward identifying the victim as female. Clues from the bones also hinted that the victim was of European descent. This does not necessarily mean the person came from Europe. It means that the victim came from a line of people who share characteristics of people who once lived in Europe.

How Tall? How Old?

Estimating the height of the person was the team's next task. Usually this is done using a formula that includes the length of the long bones and the sex of the victim. Because they were still not sure if the victim was male or female, this process was made more difficult for Galloway and her students. From their analysis of the bones, however, they believed that the victim's age was within the "forty- to sixty-year range" at the time of death.[2]

Next, the skeleton was examined to see if any injuries had occurred at the time of death. This brought Galloway back to the skull, as workers who had originally found the remains believed there was a trauma to the head. After looking at the skull, Galloway noted that there was no sign of trauma to the head. There was an opening at the base of the skull where the spinal cord passes through, and she believed this was the hole that the workers had reported.

A Cool Tool: The Mandibulometer

The mandible is a jawbone. This gadget is used for measuring the lower jaw; this information is added to the biological profile.

A Gun Wound Revealed

For the rest of the skeleton, the team used a microscope to search the bones for signs of trauma or history, like past breaks and healing. Further inspection of the femur, or thighbone, showed that the site of the past break was smooth, meaning it had healed very well. The amount of healing showed that the break had occurred at least ten years before the individual died.

How did the bone become broken? There was no clue from looking at the outside of the femur, since it had healed so perfectly. On a hunch, Galloway did a radiograph of the injury site. She was pleased to see the answer was, in fact, still inside the bone more than a hundred years later. The radiograph showed lead particles still visible in the bone. Most certainly, these had come from a gunshot wound.

Identity Uncertain

With the evidence they had, Galloway and her students still could not explain for sure how the victim had died, but the healed gunshot wound brought up the gender mystery again. This type of trauma would have been far more likely to have happened to a man than to a woman.

Galloway and her students stared at the skeleton on the table before them. Many of the dead person's features were female. However, the healed gunshot wound, the gun, the spent bullet, the pocket watch, and the whiskey bottle were clues that suggested the victim was male. The combination of research and evidence brought up an amazing idea. Could both be right? The facts suggested that if the victim was a woman, she was most likely pretending to be a man!

There may be several reasons why a woman in the late nineteenth century would choose to live as a man. Scientists can only make conclusions based on the

These forensic anthropology students are piecing together pieces of unidentified skeletal remains.

evidence they have. Galloway and her students analyzed everything they knew about this case. The forensic anthropologist then had each person on her team go through the facts, presenting a "case" based on the evidence. This process allowed each student his or her own interpretation—with the chance to defend it, too.

Galloway insisted that they all agree that the analysis was correct before each team member signed his or her name to the final report. With the victim in this case, they agreed there was no evidence that this individual's death was the result of a crime. The cause of death remains unknown, as does the mysterious reason this woman chose to live her life as a man.

Galloway related that the local historical society claimed the remains, burying the body as "one of the founding fathers of the community," despite the fact that research showed that the body was female. Alison Galloway explained that her lab could have done DNA testing to confirm the gender, but instead, did not. They thought that if "she had 'passed' as a male, she could go to the grave as she had lived."

Working on Location

Some crime scenes are more complicated than that of the mysterious "man" found near the railway tracks, particularly if the crime is recent. Experience has helped Galloway create a system to carefully examine the site and collect evidence. Usually her students accompany her. There is a lot of work to be done when recovering bodies, and all of it must be documented.

Crime scenes can be local, said Galloway. "We have had them in backyards or even under the house in a crawl space." Most often, though, the crime scenes she is called to are in remote locations. Finding them is easier if she and her team meet the police at a prearranged place and all go together. But this is not always possible, and instructions to find crime scenes are sometimes unclear if the body is in a wilderness or unpopulated area. A further problem is that cell phones often do not work in remote places.

Proceed With Caution

Recovering human remains can be dirty, smelly, and sometimes dangerous work. Most often the team wears clothes that are easily washed. Sometimes they wear disposable suits. Good boots with toe protection are necessary, as the condition of the crime scene is often unknown until they get there. Galloway's team must be ready for mud or rocks and be able to get good traction in case the crime scene is on a steep hill. In such places, they sometimes string up ropes so that no one falls. Other safety concerns include avoiding poison oak and stinging nettles, as well as rattlesnakes and scorpions. Galloway's team always carries a first aid kit to help treat injuries or exposure to poisonous plants. Insect repellent is also a must.

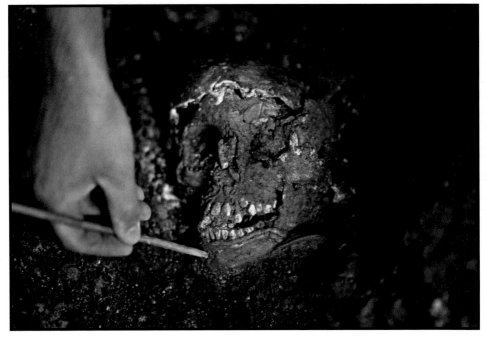

Digging up human remains must be done very carefully.

Galloway's job is to collect the body for later analysis. Because of her expertise with skeletons, this is the kind of case on which she will typically be asked to assist, particularly if the bones are scattered. Galloway explained, "It is helpful to have an anthropologist at the scene because the bones are harder to find than expected. While just about anyone can pick out a skull, finding the wrist bones among the leaves or ribs from a pile of branches is harder."

A Map to Make Sense

The team makes a grid map of the crime scene. They use string and tape measures to lay out one marked area.

Galloway and her students cross the strings to make evenly spaced squares within a larger area. A map of the grid is drawn, and bones and objects found are marked to show their exact location. This method works best if the crime scene is not too large.

More often, Galloway and her team use a total mapping station unit that produces maps on a computer. It takes longer to set up than the string method, but if the crime scene is large, such as when the remains have been scattered over a large area, it saves time in the end. Each bone or item found is listed and counted, and its location is noted on the map. Everything is photographed with a digital camera.

In the Cold, Cold Ground

A buried body requires different recovery techniques. While the team may use shovels, more often they use archaeological methods to do a thorough search of the dig site. This ensures that they do not miss anything or damage the contents of the site. Galloway uses a probe or masonry trowel on the soil surface. By doing this, she can tell if the ground is solid or loose, indicating a possible grave. Galloway said that having such experience allows them to "find the edges of the grave based on the feel of the digging."

The procedure is tricky because Galloway wants to disturb the body as little as possible at first. It is important to note—and photograph—how any objects in the grave are positioned compared to the body. Once this is done, her team uses a screen to sift the dirt and catch any small bones or objects that might be important to the case. The team particularly hopes to find such items as bullets, jewelry, clothing, or identification. These things can help investigators identify the victim, and may help solve the crime.

Get Ready to Testify

Once Galloway has concluded her analysis in a crime case, she often must testify in court. This requires some preparation. Everything related to the case must be documented so that she can refer to it in court. The "chain of custody" is important. This documentation shows that the evidence—including the body—has been treated properly and securely, and has been accounted for every moment during an investigation.

For court appearances, one must be prepared in both technical and practical ways. Scientific experts are always asked about their qualifications when they testify, so Galloway brings extra copies of her report as well as a history of her academic and work history as a forensic anthropologist. Everyday matters are not forgotten either. Galloway brings extra clothes and other personal items because testifying can often take more than one day, or there can be delays while waiting to appear in court. Waiting is a big part of court appearances. Testifying can also be difficult because the opposing attorney will challenge Galloway's findings on a case. As the anthropologist points out, "That is their job—so the

SYMES REPORT: FIGURE 4

THEBES CD: 34.JPG

Forensic anthropologist Kathy Reichs testifies in a murder trial. Presenting evidence in court is an important aspect of the forensic scientist's job.

best outcome [for them] is that they get you off the stand quickly so you don't impress the jury much."

There is little doubt that the work of the forensic anthropologist often provides critical information for solving crimes. Putting the facts together, interpreting them, and finding the cause of death are major motivators for Galloway, both in her work and in her research. "Sometimes we are able to be very close to determining the actual sequence of events, and that is very encouraging."

Justice for the Dead

Galloway finds her work rewarding when forensic science helps identify the dead and helps bring those responsible for the death to justice. However, Galloway believes future forensic anthropologists need to recognize that this career is not the exciting one portrayed on television. "Do not expect [forensic work] to be glamorous," she warns.

While solving the mystery of a death is satisfying for Galloway, there is more to it than that. She finds it gratifying to "help someone who is now beyond help. We come to respect our subjects and want resolution for them."

These ideas have led Galloway to become involved with ethical issues about respecting the dignity of the dead in forensic science. In the case of the skeletal remains found by the railway tracks, a community came forward to bury the body. But if this is not the case, how

Dr. Galloway examines bones in her lab.

should skeletal remains be stored? Often they are kept in boxes. Should something more be done to honor them? Should human remains be put on display? These are the kinds of questions she is exploring. In her own cases, she wants a respectful ending wherever possible. Whether this includes a murder conviction or returning the remains to the family, Galloway concludes, "It feels good to 'settle' them somewhere."

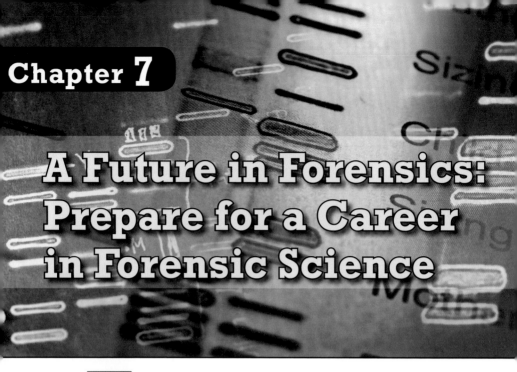

Chapter 7

A Future in Forensics: Prepare for a Career in Forensic Science

Are you a puzzle-solver? Are you fascinated by science? Do you share traits with any of the scientists profiled in this book? If you are like those scientists, you have a strong work ethic, a keen attention to detail, and a strong background in science. If you're serious about pursuing employment in this field, you should focus studies on the natural sciences. General and organic chemistry, biology, physics, calculus, and statistics can all build a foundation mastering the knowledge required for this career.

Many colleges and universities now offer degree programs in forensic science. There are associate's, bachelor's, master's and doctorate degrees available. To check if a program is reputable, check with the American Academy of Forensic Science and the Forensic Science Education Programs Accreditation Commission, which lists schools that are highly regarded. Also, the National

Institute of Justice, a division of the US Department of Justice, provides guidelines for model undergraduate and graduate forensic science degree programs.

Higher education programs in forensics focus on building the problem-solving skills, analytical thinking, and special training needed to succeed in the field. Graduate students in a dedicated forensics degree program will learn about crime scenes, physical evidence, applicable law, and science. Class work also stresses ethics and professional responsibility.

Medical investigators often have a university degree or a combination of police and medical backgrounds.

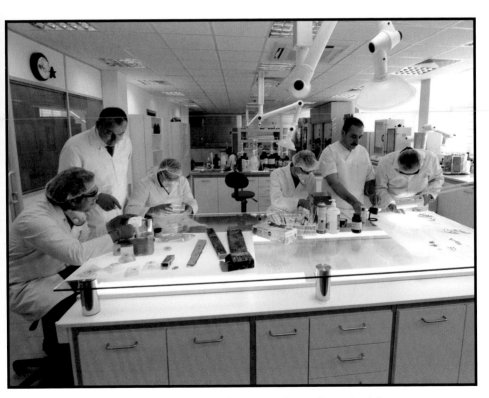

Fingerprint identification specialists at work in a forensics laboratory.

Careers such as latent print examiners or morgue technicians require less formal education.

Salaries in the field of forensic science cover a broad range. The Bureau of Labor Statistics (BLS) reports that the average annual salary for a forensic science technician was about $57,000 in 2013. Top earners can make as much as $90,000 a year, according to the BLS. Earnings depend on years of experience and degree attained.[1]

New technologies are constantly being developed that help forensic scientists identify bodies and suspects. The ability to identify potential criminals by small bits of DNA is helping solve more and more crimes. If you're interested in cutting-edge science and have a bit of detective in you, you might want to consider pursuing a career path in forensic science.

Words of Advice From the Experts

Heidi Robbins, Senior Criminalist:

"If you want to be a forensic scientist, you need to be a strong student overall, but particularly in math and science. Also, you must have a college degree for this job, so at a young age, you must prepare yourself with a school curriculum that lends itself to college or university admission. The ability to be comfortable speaking in front of people is also a desirable skill for a criminalist. Such things as the debate team or speech club could help with your public speaking skills."[2]

Dr. Sam Andrews, Forensic Pathologist:

Andrews suggests that students focus on the sciences in school, particularly biology and chemistry. He strongly believes that anyone interested in a career in medicine needs to get experience in the field. As a student, volunteering in a hospital is the best way to do this. Once in college, students should try to volunteer with a physician. Students must understand that becoming a forensic pathologist will not happen overnight. "The time commitment is the biggest thing they have to realize. After high school I went to school for fourteen additional years."[3]

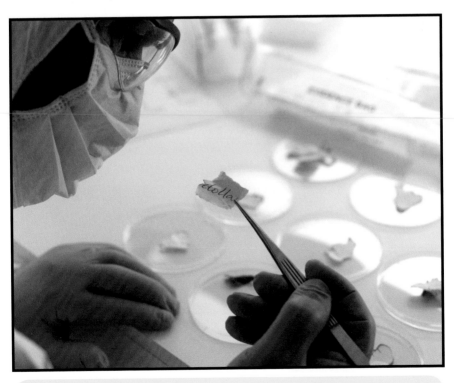

A forensic scientist studies paper evidence from a crime.

Dr. Gail Anderson, Forensic Entomologist:

"Get a solid science background in the area of interest, do not try to be a generalist. Do not try to leap into forensic science until you have a strong scientific background in your own science first."[4]

Dr. Ed Espinoza, Forensic Chemist:

"If kids already have an ability to be a good mathematician, biologist, or chemist, they should consider wildlife forensic science to be a way to use skills they already possess. Once they have the studies, focus on analytical skills, pursue that, then later focus on forensics. That is, be a chemist first."[5]

A researcher examines DNA in a forensics laboratory.

Dr. Elizabeth Rega, Physical Anthropologist:
"Take science classes such as evolutionary biology, anatomy, physics, and statistics. Find a researcher whose work you like and volunteer in the lab, field, or museum."[6]

Dr. Alison Galloway, Forensic Anthropologist:
"I would advise junior high students to focus on their science classes. They could also see if there is a crime lab in the area that allows tours and organize one. Starting in high school, they should really hit the science classes—biology, anatomy, and chemistry, in particular. Absolutely essential is keeping out of trouble!"[7]

Get a Jumpstart

For students still in primary, middle, and high school, work hard at math and core sciences, like biology, chemistry, and physics. Learn about animals and keep up with changes in computer technology. Visit your local library, because reading about forensic science is something you can do today. And stay curious, because regardless of how much education is required, curiosity is perhaps the most important quality that all forensic scientists share!

Appendix: Forensic Scientists: Jobs at a Glance[1]

CRIMINALIST/FORENSIC SCIENTIST	
Education Required	Bachelor of science degree; many have master's degree and some have PhDs
Salary Range*	$33,610 - $91,400

FORENSIC PATHOLOGIST	
Education Required	Bachelor of science degree; doctor of medicine degree (MD); five-year residency in anatomical pathology; one-year fellowship in forensic pathology
Salary Range[2]	$80,000 - $200,000

FORENSIC ENTOMOLOGIST	
Education Required	Bachelor of science degree; master's degree; PhD
Salary Range	$42,480 - $115,260

FORENSIC CHEMIST	
Education Required	Bachelor of science degree; master's degree; PhD
Salary Range	$41,560 - $126,220

PHYSICAL/FORENSIC ANTHROPOLOGIST	
Education Required	Bachelor's degree; master's degree; PhD
Salary Range	$34,580 - $93,650

IDENTIFICATION OFFICER	
Education Required	Typically, must work as a police officer for at least three years, upon acceptance to become an identification officer, extensive courses, testing, and on-the-job training required. College preferred in science and/or forensics program.
Salary Range	$33,030 - $92,450

[1] Source for all careers except Forensic Pathologist: Bureau of Labor Statistics, *Occupational Outlook Handbook, 2014–15 Edition*, May 2013, US Department of Labor, http://www.bls.gov/oes/current/oes_stru.htm.

[2] "Forensic Pathologist Career," http://www.itsgov.com/forensic-pathologist-salary-requirements-education.html.

*Salary figures will vary according to job specifications, geographic location, and market demands.

Chapter Notes

Chapter 1. A Tale of Telltale Clues

1. Jonathan Hayes, personal interview, March 19, 2015. All quotes from Hayes come from this interview.
2. Sam Andrews, personal interview, April 18, 2008. All quotes from Andrews come from this interview.

Chapter 2. Death in a Dumpster

1. Aurelio Locsin, "Forensic Scientist vs. Criminalists," *Houston Chronicle*, accessed April 21, 2015, <http://work.chron.com/forensic-scientists-vs-criminalists-21410.html>.
2. Indianapolis-Marion County Forensic Services Agency, "Latent Print Examiner," accessed October 16, 2008, <http://www.indygov.org/eGov/County/FSA/Disciplines/latent_examiner.htm>.
3. Heidi Robbins, personal interview, August 1, 2007. Unless otherwise indicated, all quotes from Robbins come from this interview. Robbins reviewed information and provided updates on March 23, 2015.

Chapter 3. Bugging Out to Fight Crime

1. Gail S. Anderson, "Forensic Entomology: The Use of Insects in Death Investigations," *Case Studies in Forensic Anthropology*, S. Fairgreave, ed. (Toronto: Charles C. Thomas, 1999), 1–12.
2. Gail Anderson, e-mail correspondence with author, June 1, 2007. Unless otherwise indicated, all quotes from Anderson come from this e-mail.
3. Anderson, "Forensic Entomology."
4. Gail Anderson, e-mail correspondence with author, July 22, 2008.
5. Anderson, "Forensic Entomology."
6. Ibid.

7. Canada AM – CTV Television, Broadcast Script, Toronto, Canada, March 19, 2001.

8. Anderson, "Forensic Entomology."

9. "The Cheese Skipper," MSN Encarta, accessed October 16, 2008, <http://encarta.msn.com/encyclopedia_761584521/Cheese_Skipper.html>.

10. Gail Anderson, "August 2006: Forensic Investigations in the Saanich Inlet," *Research Highlights: The Venus Project*, accessed October 16, 2008, <http://www. venus.uvic.ca/>.

11. Ibid.

12. Gail Anderson and Canadian Chemical News, "Forensics Overboard," November/December 2006, 14–15.

Chapter 4. The Case of the Walruses That Lost Their Heads

1. The National Park Service, "Bering Land Bridge National Preserve," *Prehistory of Alaska*, accessed October 16, 2008, <http://www.nps.gov/akso/ akarc/cr_bela.htm>.

2. Alaska Department of Fish and Game, "The Walrus," December 17, 2007, <http://www.adfg.state.ak.us/pubs/notebook/marine/walrus.php>.

3. Edgar O. Espinoza et al., "Taphonomic Indicators Used to Infer Wasteful Subsistence Hunting in Northwest Alaska," *Anthropozoologica* 2526, 1997, 103–112.

4. U.S. Department of the Interior, "The U.S. Fish and Wildlife Service Forensics Lab," September 23, 2008, <http://www.lab.fws.gov/>.

5. Espinoza, et al.

6. Ed Espinoza, telephone interview, May 16, 2007.

7. Ed Espinoza, telephone interview, May 16, 2007. Unless otherwise indicated, all quotes from Espinoza come from this interview.

Chapter 5. A Dinosaur Detective

1. Elizabeth Rega, e-mail correspondence with author, April 21, 2007. Unless otherwise indicated, all quotes from Rega come from this e-mail.

2. Elizabeth Rega and Robert Holmes, "Manual Pathology Indicative of Locomotor Behavior in Two Chasmosaurine Dinosaurs," *Society of Vertebrate Paleontology Presentation*, October 2006.

3. Stefan Thompson and Robert Holmes, "Forelimb Stance and Step Cycle in *Chasmosaurus irvinensis* (Dinosauria: Neoceratopsia)". *Palaeontologia Electronica* 10, Issue 1, 2007, 1–17.

4. Ibid.

5. The Field Museum, "Sue's Vital Statistics," *Sue at the Field Museum*, 2007, <http://www.fieldmuseum.org/sue/about_vital .asp>.

6. Gregory M. Erickson et al., "Gigantism and Comparative Life-History Parameters of Tyrannosaurid Dinosaurs," *Nature* 430, 2004, 772–775.

7. Elizabeth Rega, e-mail correspondence with author, April 23, 2007.

8. Chris Brochu, "Osteology of *Tyrannosaurus rex*: Insights from a Nearly Complete Skeleton and High-Resolution Computed Tomographic Analysis of the Skull," *Memoir 7, Society of Vertebrate Paleontology*, 2003, 116.

9. Elizabeth Rega, e-mail correspondence with author, April 23, 2007.

10. Ibid.

Chapter 6. The Puzzle of the Perplexing Person

1 Alison Galloway, e-mail correspondence with author, May 11, 2007. Unless otherwise indicated, all quotes from Galloway come from this e-mail.

2. Alison Galloway, e-mail correspondence with author, May 27, 2008.

Chapter 7. A Future in Forensics: Prepare for a Career in Forensic Science

1. "Forensic Science Technicians: Occupational Employment and Wages, May 2013" *Bureau of Labor Statistics*, accessed March 23, 2015, <http://www.bls.gov/oes/current/oes194092.htm>.

2. Heidi Robbins, e-mail correspondence with author, July 30, 2007.

3. Sam Andrews, personal interview, April 18, 2008.

4. Gail Anderson, e-mail correspondence with author, June 1, 2007.

5. Ed Espinoza, telephone interview, May 16, 2007.

6. Elizabeth Rega, e-mail correspondence with author, April 23, 2007.

7. Alison Galloway, e-mail correspondence with author, May 11, 2007.

Glossary

accelerant—A substance (like gasoline) that is used to help spread a fire.

anthropophagy—Animals that eat the flesh of humans.

arson—A fire started intentionally. Committing arson is a crime.

arthropod—An animal with a hard exterior skeleton and jointed legs. This group includes crabs, centipedes, spiders, and insects.

autopsy—An examination of a corpse done to determine the cause of death, looking at both the outside and inside of a body by dissecting it.

bindle—A piece of paper folded to securely hold trace evidence. Also called a pharmaceutical fold, or druggist's fold.

biological fluids—Any fluid that comes from the body, such as saliva, sweat, blood, and urine.

bunions—A deformity caused by structural problems with the foot or by wearing shoes that are too tight.

cadaver—The dead body of a human.

callus—A thickened area of bone or tissue.

chronic condition—A condition that is continuous, or keeps returning over a long period of time.

corpse—The dead body of a human or animal.

decedent—A dead person.

decompose—To break down or decay.

DNA (deoxyribonucleic acid)—Genetic material found in the cells of organisms. It is made of two chains of nucleotides in the form of a double helix.

femur—The thighbone.

forensics—The use of science to help solve crimes and medical mysteries.

gait—The way an animal or human walks or runs.

grid—A series of perpendicular lines that intersect at regular intervals to form small squares within a larger staked area; it is used for mapping locations within crime scenes.

homicide—The killing of one human being by another.

hypothermia—An abnormally low body temperature that can cause death.

ice floes—Large flat chunks of ice that float in the ocean.

ligaments—Strong tissues that connect bones or cartilage.

lug—The raised part of a boot tread that provides extra traction.

manus—Hand.

osteomyelitis—An infection that causes an inflammation of the bone with pain, redness, and swelling.

paleopathology—The study of changes from diseases, injuries, or abnormalities in fossils.

pelagic hunting—Hunting in the open sea.

perpetrator—Someone who commits a crime.

predation—The act of one organism feeding on another, often by killing it first.

radiograph—A photograph taken using radiation such as x-rays or gamma rays.

stereomicroscope—A large microscope that can be moved at different angles to view objects too large for regular microscopes.

subsistence hunting—Hunting in which the meat is harvested.

toxicology—The study of the effects of chemicals on the human body, particularly drugs and poisons.

trauma—An injury.

Further Reading

Books

Ford, Jean. *Forensics in American Culture.* Broomall, Pa.: Mason Crest, 2013.

Mooney, Carla. *Forensics.* White River Junction, Vt.: Nomad Press, 2013.

Murray, Elizabeth. *Forensic Identification: Putting a Name and Face on Death.* Minneapolis: Twenty-First Century, 2012.

Solway, Andrew. *The Human Body: Investigating an Unexplained Death.* Chicago: Heinemann, 2013.

Walker, Maryalice. *Pathology.* Broomall, Penn.: Mason Crest, 2013.

Woog, Adam. *Careers in Forensic Science.* New York: Cavendish Square, 2014.

Video

***Forensics on Trial.* PBS Video, 2012. Running time 53:10.**
video.pbs.org/video/2290878958/

Web Sites

aafs.org/students/student-career/choosing-career
The American Academy of Forensic Sciences

lab.fws.gov/students.php
The U.S. Fish and Wildlife Service Forensics Laboratory

www.virtualmuseum.ca/sgc-cms/expositions-exhibitions/detective-investigator/en/
Virtual Exhibit on Forensic Science

Index

A

analytical forensic chemist
  education/training, 116–117
  job description, 79
  lab analysis, 63, 77
  procedure/test development,
    70–71
Anderson, Gail, 46–48, 50–53,
  55–58, 60–62, 116
Andrews, Sam, 21–26, 115
animal forensic science
  crime scene investigation, 58,
    60, 63–67
  dangers in, 73–75
  job description, 78–79
  lab analysis, 75–78
  procedure/test development,
    70–73
  qualifications, 78–79
anthropophagy, 61
autopsies, 10–12, 22–23, 26, 47–48,
  52, 93
  cause of death determi-
    nation, 10–11, 13–14
  disease detection via, 10, 13, 48
  external examination, 11–12
  internal examination, 12–13
  limitations of, 27
  medical history, 21–23, 25–26
  preparation for, 10–11
  tools, 12–13

B

bindles, 38
biological evidence, 37
biological profile, 99, 102
bite wounds, 91–92
blood/bloodstains
  evidence collection, 15–17, 28,
    33, 36–37
  lab analysis, 13–14, 22–23,
    41–42, 45
  pattern matching, 34–35, 39, 41
blowflies, 46, 53–54, 57–58, 61
bones. *See also* forensic anthropology
  cleaning, 98–99
  height determination, 101
  measuring, 99–101, 102,
    106–107
  sex determination, 100–101
  trauma, 89, 91, 93, 101–103
Brochu, Chris, 88

C

cadavers, dissection of, 81–85
calipers, 99–100
cause of death determination
  autopsy, 6, 12–14, 22, 25, 36,
    91, 104, 110
  forensic anthropologists, 93–94
Chasmosaurus, 81–83, 86–87
chemical burns, 21, 23, 25
Crane, Al, 63
crime scene investigation
  autopsies in, 10–13
criminalists, 8, 30–31
  animal forensics, 58, 63, 78–79
  education/training, 45, 114
  evidence kits, 37–38
  forensic anthropologists,
    61–62, 95–96, 104–108
  forensic chemistry, 33, 63, 116
  hazards, 10, 31–34, 48,
    105–106
  job description, 6–8
  mapping, 106–107
  photography, 10–11, 31–32, 34,
    38, 41, 96, 107–108
cross-contamination prevention,
  48, 50

D

datalogger, 52

decomposition, 19, 47, 58, 60
defensive wounds, 35
dental records, 26
disease, 5, 10, 13, 48, 81–82, 89,
  93–94. See also infection,
  detecting
DNA analysis, 6–7, 15–16, 26, 41,
  71, 104, 114

E

Espinoza, Ed, 63–79, 116
evidence
  biological, 37
  chain of custody, 108, 110
  impression, 35, 38–39
  preparation for court, 17,
    26–27, 43–45, 50, 56–58, 77,
    108, 110
  trace, 14, 38, 42, 95–96
evidence collection
  autopsies, 10–17, 22, 52–53
  crime scene investigation, 32,
    34, 37–39, 41, 71, 104–108
  insects, 46–48, 50–58
  specialists required, 28, 32, 43,
    73
  tools, 37–38

F

fingerprints, 8, 25–26, 32–33, 38, 71
footprints
  analysis, 38, 86
  collection of, 32
forensic anthropology. See also
  bones; paleopathology.
  buried body recovery, 107–108
  cause of death determination,
    93–94, 97–99
  crime scene investigation,
    95–96, 104–108
  education/training, 117
  identification of remains,
    95–98, 105–108
  job description, 95–96,

  110–111
  lab analysis, 97–98, 104
forensic entomology
  education/training, 116
  evidence collection, 48, 50–58
  job description, 46–48
  lab analysis, 52–53
  water-associated deaths, 58,
    60–62
forensic identification specialist
  (FIS), 28
forensic pathologists. See also
  autopsies
  animal forensics, 58, 60–62,
    78–79
  education/training, 5–8, 115
  job description, 5–8, 10–12, 17,
    22, 25–27
forensic science described, 6–8,
  112–114

G

Galloway, Alison, 95–111, 117

H

Hayes, Jonathan, 5–8, 10–17
height determination, 101
Holmes, Rob, 86–87
homicides, 6–8, 12, 25, 28, 34, 36,
  48, 58, 61–62

I

identification officers, 51
identification of remains, 58, 61, 68,
  93, 95–101, 104–107, 110–111
impression evidence, 35, 38–39, 96
infection, detecting, 83, 90, 93. See
  also disease.

L

latent print examiners, 32, 114

M

maggots, 46, 50–52, 54–55, 57
medical history, 10, 21–24
medical photographer, 10–11
mitochondrial DNA, 16–17
morgue technicians, 10–12, 114

P

paleopathology. *See also* forensic
  anthropology.
  cause of injury determination,
    81–87
  described, 81, 94
  education/training, 117
pelagic hunting, 67
petechial hemorrhage, 8, 10
photography
  animal forensics, 64–66
  of autopsy, 10–11
  of crime scene, 32, 34, 38, 41,
    96, 107–108
  injury source determination,
    81–82, 85–86
  in stride determination, 85–87
  as testimony, 43–45

R

Rega, Elizabeth, 80–83, 85–94, 117
remotely operated submersible
  vehicle (ROPOS ROV), 60–62
Robbins, Heidi, 28, 30–39, 41–45,
  114

S

salaries, 114. *See also* Appendix
salt level testing, 22–25
search warrants, 36, 38
seizure, 21–22
serologist, 41–42
sex determination, 100–101
stereomicroscopes, 42
subsistence hunting, 65–66, 73

T

temperature, 27, 50, 52–55, 74
testimony
  criminalists, 30–31, 70–71
  evidence preparation, 26, 45
  forensic anthropologists, 108,
    110
  forensic entomology, 56–58
  medical examiners, 26
  procedure/test development, 45
time of death determination
  autopsy, 13–14, 27
  forensic anthropologists, 101
  insects and, 47–48, 50, 53, 55,
    57–58, 60, 62
Tirabosso, Alex, 86–87
toxicology, 13–14, 23–25
trace evidence, 14, 38, 42, 95–96
Tyrannosaurus rex, 87–93

V

Victoria Experimental Network Under the Sea (VENUS), 60–62

X

x-rays, 12, 26, 89